Teach Yourself®

KU-018-573

KANT
A Complete Introduction

Robert L. Wicks

First published in Great Britain in 2014 by Hodder & Stoughton. An Hachette UK company.

First published in US in 2014 by The McGraw-Hill Companies, Inc.

Copyright © Robert Wicks 2014

The right of Robert Wicks to be identified as the Author of the Work has been asserted by him in accordance with the Copyright, Designs and Patents Act 1988.

Database right Hodder & Stoughton (makers)

The *Teach Yourself* name is a registered trademark of Hachette UK.

British Library Cataloguing in Publication Data: a catalogue record for this title is available from the British Library.

Library of Congress Catalog Card Number: on file.

ISBN 978 1 444 19126 4

eISBN 978 1 444 19128 8

10 9 8 7 6 5 4 3

The publisher has used its best endeavours to ensure that any website addresses referred to in this book are correct and active at the time of going to press. However, the publisher and the author have no responsibility for the websites and can make no guarantee that a site will remain live or that the content will remain relevant, decent or appropriate.

The publisher has made every effort to mark as such all words which it believes to be trademarks. The publisher should also like to make it clear that the presence of a word in the book, whether marked or unmarked, in no way affects its legal status as a trademark.

Every reasonable effort has been made by the publisher to trace the copyright holders of material in this book. Any errors or omissions should be notified in writing to the publisher, who will endeavour to rectify the situation for any reprints and future editions.

Cover image © iStockPhoto

Typeset by Cenveo® Publisher Services.

Printed and bound in Great Britain by CPI Group (UK) Ltd., Croydon, CR0 4YY.

John Murray Learning policy is to use papers that are natural, renewable and recyclable products and made from wood grown in sustainable forests. The logging and manufacturing processes are expected to conform to the environmental regulations of the country of origin.

John Murray Learning

338 Euston Road

London NW1 3BH

www.hodder.co.uk

KANT
A Complete Introduction

To Valentina, my courageous daughter

Robert L. Wicks is an Associate Professor of Philosophy at the University of Auckland, New Zealand. He is the author of *Kant On Judgement* (2007), along with books on Schopenhauer, Hegel, Nietzsche, Modern French Philosophy and European Aesthetics.

Contents

Introduction

Immanuel Kant's philosophy is one of the most profound and influential ever to have been written. It is also among the more complicated philosophies, where each technical term compares to a part of a car's engine, where all of the parts are intended to work in harmony to produce a smoothly running mechanism. As Kant composed it, a few of his philosophy's 'parts' do not fit with each other perfectly, and it has become the business of contemporary Kant scholars to redesign these parts to produce a more thoroughly coherent and persuasive Kantian philosophy. In this book, our goal will be to describe the classical design of Kant's philosophical 'engine' as he intended it, the kind of historical terrain upon which it was supposed to run, and the spiritual destination towards which it was meant to take us.

Kant was writing during the late 1700s, and at the forefront of his theorizing were problems generated by religion, science and morality. These themes define the intellectual atmosphere of his thought. At the most basic level is the problem of how we can be free, if scientific thought can predict everything that happens. We have all wondered about, and perhaps dreamed or even feared, what it would be like, if science were perfect and we could predict all that will happen. Kant considered this, and then became puzzled about what would become of God and our sense of morality. How can one blame or praise someone, if their actions at age 80 were already knowable when they were only three years old? The problem of freedom versus determinism is at the centre of Kant's philosophy.

Perhaps you have heard of Kant only in passing and were curious about what his philosophy actually says. Perhaps you are a student studying Kant who would like to read a book that explains his views briefly, but also accurately, reliably, memorably and easily. Perhaps you are a specialist in a field other than philosophy who has encountered some interesting references to Kant's philosophy. Perhaps you studied Kant once, long ago, and would like to refresh your memory of his central ideas. This book is written for you. It aims to be self-contained and self-explanatory, such that no background in philosophy will be necessary to understand it. The relevant background ideas will be provided as we go along.

Kant is known mainly from three main books that he wrote, each of whose titles begins with the word 'critique'. These books are frequently referred to as Kant's three 'critiques' and his philosophy is often called, appropriately, the 'critical philosophy'. This book will thus have a part devoted to each of Kant's *Critiques*. The first *Critique* is concerned with the question of truth. The second, with the question of goodness. The third is concerned with beauty. Residing accordingly at the core of Kant's philosophy and guiding our study of it will be truth, goodness and beauty – the most famous triad in the history of Western philosophy.

We will focus upon Kant's three *Critiques* in light of Kant's own statement at the end of the first *Critique*, of three questions that cover all of our interests insofar as we are rational beings. These are:

1 What can I know?

2 What ought I to do?

3 What may I hope?

We will consequently look at Kant's theory of knowledge, his moral theory, and his aesthetic and political theory, especially insofar as they bear on our moral destination. Kant's third question is about what we may hope, if we do our duty and consequently deserve happiness. It concerns the ideal, peaceful world that awaits, if everyone were to realize their potential as rational beings.

Our book's title is *Kant – A Complete Introduction*. It aims at completeness in the modest sense of trying to cover the key aspects of Kant's philosophy. Thousands of books have been written on Kant's philosophy, many of which have stimulated further books on Kant in their wake. In this respect, his thought continues to live and grow, expanding our horizons to defy any sense of completeness.

It will help to mention here at the outset, that the quotations from Kant have been taken from editions in the public domain and/or have been translated by the present author. In the field of Kant scholarship, the standard way to refer to quotes from the *Critique of Pure Reason*, is to cite the edition and page number after the quote. The first edition (1781) is signified by the letter 'A'; the second edition (1787), by the letter 'B'. A reference that reads 'A51/B75', for example, signifies that the original German passage is located in the first edition on page 51, and in the second edition on page 75. We will follow this standard format in our text, as we investigate how powerful the human mind really is.

How to use this book

This Complete Introduction from Teach Yourself ® includes a number of special boxed features, which have been developed to help you understand the subject more quickly and remember it more effectively. Throughout the book you will find these indicated by the following icons:

The book includes concise **quotes** from the philosopher under discussion in each chapter. They are referenced so that you can include them in essays if you are unable to get your hands on the source.

The **key ideas** are highlighted throughout the chapters, and distil the most important points and thoughts. If you have only half an hour to go before an exam, scanning through these would be a very good way of spending your time.

The **study questions** at the end of each chapter are designed to help you ensure that you have taken in the most important concepts from the chapter. Answers are not supplied, as the questions are intended to be starting points for further study.

The **spotlight** boxes offer interesting or amusing anecdotes to help bring the philosophers and their ideas to life.

The **dig deeper** boxes give you ways to explore topics in greater depth than is possible in this introductory level book.

Section One:

Background

1

Life and writings

Philosophies may aim for universality, but none are written in a vacuum. Philosophers are flesh-and-blood people – eating, drinking, laughing, reflecting, and slowly aging – living at a particular historical time and inevitably absorbing the values, concerns and overall atmosphere of their surrounding culture.

In this chapter, we will survey Kant's life (1724–1804), the bulk of which extended across the 1700s into the dawn of the industrial age. As was true for René Descartes (1596–1650), the father of modern philosophy, the conflicting forces of science and religion shaped Kant's outlook. The impressive exactitude and predictive power of Newtonian physics, as it stood in perplexing contrast to our sense of moral value and freedom, created a tension that Kant took a lifetime to resolve.

Kant did not grow up at the centre of an empire, with the excitement and cultural opportunities that one might enjoy in Rome, Paris or London; however, as a seaport on the Baltic and the capital city of East Prussia, neither was Konigsberg completely isolated. Today, his hometown remains on a strategically important coastal area, set within a small segment of Russian land tucked between Lithuania and Poland. The city was named Kaliningrad in 1946 upon its absorption into the Soviet Union after World War II, but for most of its existence it was known as Königsberg. During Kant's time, its population was approximately 50,000.

For most of Kant's life, the Kingdom of Prussia, of which East Prussia was a part, was ruled by Frederick II, who reigned from 1740–1786, when Kant was ages 16 to 62. Frederick the Great, as he was known, in addition to being an extraordinary military tactician, was an intellectually and artistically sophisticated sovereign whose advocacy of religious tolerance sustained a productive environment for intellectuals. Most of the kingdom's inhabitants were favourably disposed to Frederick, and Kant was no exception. He dedicated to the king his 1755 work, *Universal Natural History and Theory of the Heavens*, and later spoke well of him in his 1784 essay, 'Answer to the Question: What is Enlightenment?' During the years of his early philosophical development and into the middle of the later period of his writings for which he is most famous, Kant's interest in philosophy was not significantly threatened by the political conditions at large. The situation became less reliable in 1786, when Frederick's successor, Frederick William II, assumed control.

By the time Kant was born in 1724, Lutheranism had been prevailing in the German-speaking world for a couple of centuries, ever since the days of Martin Luther (1483–1546). Kant himself was exposed to Pietism, a specific version of Lutheranism, which was then dominating in social institutions, well into his adult years. Kant's family was devoutly Pietist, the clergyman who supported and supervised his early education was Pietist, and the schools that he attended were committed to conveying Pietist values. Pietism itself advocated a devotional, emotion-centred approach to God, forgiveness towards others, and a practical community awareness. In its more extreme forms, it was fanatical and anti-scientific, two qualities for which Kant later expressed abhorrence.

Kant's relationship to Pietism was consequently mixed. He loved his mother, who was steeped in the religion, and who, given her intelligence and good character, displayed to him the best of what Pietism had to offer. On the other hand, Pietism does not loom large in Kant's philosophy. He instead had an unwavering respect for rules, laws, regulations, mathematics and reason that kept him at a distance from emotional, subjectively oriented solutions to metaphysical and moral issues. He nonetheless retained a place for faith in his philosophy, admitting that understanding and reason have no power to reveal ultimate truth. In this respect Pietistic sentiments towards metaphysical matters are not excluded.

The severe conditions of Kant's early Pietist education alone, though, were sufficient to dampen any reasonable child's enthusiasm towards the religion. Although the initial grammar school which he attended from ages six to seven was staffed by a Pietist instructor, the Collegium Fridericianum, which he attended from ages eight to fifteen, worked Kant particularly hard, requiring him to attend school six days a week with a heavy study load.

With an emphasis upon religion and languages, scientific subjects took a back seat, but Kant nonetheless received an outstanding education in Latin, as well as in Greek, Hebrew and French, which served him well in later years. Scholarly treatises were still being written in Latin as a rule, so a thorough knowledge of this language was still essential for success in the academic world. It is revealing that Kant declined to attend religious ceremonies of any kind throughout his adult life, even when he was presiding over the university, when as a formality, he was sometimes expected to attend.

Key idea: Pietism:

Kant was raised in a Pietist family and educated in Pietist schools. As an adult, he did not identify with organized religion, but his unwavering faith in morality remained at the foundation of his philosophy.

Kant came from a family of socially respectable artisans associated with the harness-maker and saddle-maker guilds, where his father often made a healthy living, notwithstanding some periods of struggle, bordering on poverty. The death of Kant's mother at age 40, when Kant was 13 years old, precipitated some hardship. Her death left his father with an 18-year-old daughter, Regina Dorothea (1719–1792), 13-year-old Kant, three younger daughters, Maria Elisabeth (1727–1796), age ten, Anna Luise (1730–1774), age seven, Katharina Barbara (1731–1807), age six, and a two-year-old son, Johann Heinrich (1735–1800). Most of Kant's siblings lived into old age, aside from Anna Luise, who died at age 34. Kant's mother gave birth to at least nine children in all, losing at least three in their infancy, two prior to Kant's own birth. This made him the first son to survive and the head of the family after his parents died.

At age 16, Kant entered the University of Königsberg, where one of his lecturers, Martin Knutzen (1713–1751), introduced him to Newtonian physics as well as to the then-prevalent Leibnizian philosophy of Christian Wolff (1679–1754), which was inspired by Gottfried Wilhelm Leibniz (1646–1716). Both influenced Kant. Knutzen was also interested in the British empiricist philosophers such as John Locke, whose work he was translating into German at the end of his short life.

During Kant's university studies and in the years of his early career, the influence of Newtonian physics was strong. His initial publications were straightforwardly scientific, and focused on issues related to physics, terrestrial forces and astronomy in genuine scientific detail. The Wolffian influence also remained: as a professor at the University of Königsberg years later, Kant taught from textbooks written by Wolffians such as Alexander Baumgarten (1714–1762), whose work influenced Kant's aesthetic theory, and Georg Friedrich Meier (1718–1777), whose logic textbook he used.

It is perhaps surprising to hear that Kant did not graduate from the university, where he studied for eight years from 1740–1748. The reasons are unclear. We do know that his family was struggling economically when he began his studies, that his father suffered a stroke four years later, and died within two years in March, 1746, when Kant was about to turn 22. As head of the family, Kant arranged for his siblings' new lodgings, and by 1748, he had withdrawn from the university without a degree.

Kant might also have had academic reasons to withdraw. Although his 1746 manuscript, 'Thoughts on the True Estimation of Living Forces', was supervised by a professor of physics named Teske – and later dedicated to a professor of medicine when it was published as Kant's first book three years later – Kant's influential philosophy teacher, Martin Knutzen, might have had some misgivings about the manuscript or tensions with Kant himself. Knutzen does not mention Kant as one of his students. We also know that Knutzen favoured students other than Kant. Nor does Kant mention Knutzen in his writings, although he attended all of his classes.

After leaving the university, Kant worked as a tutor to the children in families in the countryside surrounding Königsberg. For six years, 1748–1754, between the ages of 24 and 30, he tutored in two, and possibly three, different families whose heads were, respectively, a pastor, a landowner and an aristocrat. Continuing his preparations to receive his degree, Kant appears to have devoted himself exactingly to the study of Newton's physics while he was away from the university for these several years. We can infer this from the contents of the book he published in 1755, upon his return to the university, *Universal Natural History and Theory of the Heavens*, which, as the title suggests, is a scientific work about the nature of the cosmos. The book's subtitle is even more revealing: 'An Essay on the Constitution and Mechanical Origin of the Entire Structure of the Universe Based on Newtonian Principles'.

Kant's book is noteworthy for its bold attempt to provide a purely mechanical account of the origin of the universe, as is done by contemporary physicists. It is also famous for containing one of the first contemporary formulations of the nebular hypothesis of the solar system's origins – the idea that the solar system was formed by a primitive cloud of matter that coalesced through the action of elementary forces. Prior to Kant, the Swedish scientist, philosopher and mystic, Emanuel Swedenborg (1688–1772) advanced a similar nebular hypothesis in 1734, two decades earlier, although Kant is often given credit for having first imagined the idea.

Coincidentally, 1755 was also the year of the devastating Lisbon earthquake, which did much to fuel the problem of how a benevolent God could allow such disasters. Kant immediately wrote three articles about the earthquake, describing it in a manner consistent with his nebular hypothesis as an event due to natural causes. With respect to evil, Kant's view is that we are in no position to judge the overall morality of these kinds of event. He notes that building cities on earthquake-susceptible land is a human decision, and that perhaps the horrors of the earthquake will motivate people towards the good end of refraining from violence when the choice is indeed in their hands, such as in decisions to wage war.

More fundamental than his discussions of the nebular hypothesis and the nature of earthquakes is the general role of scientific thought in Kant's philosophy. It can be said that his philosophy is one written by a morally conscious scientist – primarily an astronomer and geophysicist – who is fascinated by the presence and operation of natural laws. As mentioned, Kant rejects emotional solutions to philosophical problems in favour of purely rule-oriented solutions that are universally applicable, and as rock-solid as the natural laws. To appreciate the importance of natural law in his thought, note how Kant describes the supreme idea of morality in his *Groundwork of the Metaphysics of Morals* (1785). He takes natural law as the paradigm for other disciplines, stating within the sphere of morality, 'Act as though the maxim of your action were, by your will, to become a *universal law of nature*' (Section Two).

Often overshadowed by the *Critique of Pure Reason* and the works that followed thereafter, Kant's early writings show that he was an astronomer at heart, enamoured of the starry skies and their attendant natural laws of operation. This is a key to understanding the consistently rule-oriented disposition of his philosophy that finds its expression in a series of complementary clusters of law-like principles. We see this exemplified in a familiar quotation from the conclusion to the *Critique of Practical Reason*: 'Two things fill the mind with always new and increasing admiration and awe, the more often and more steadily one thinks about them: the starry heavens above me and the moral law within me'.

Key idea: Laws of nature:

Kant respected the idea that nature operates predictably according to a set of universal laws. Underlying not only his discussions of physical phenomena such as earthquakes and the origin of the solar system, the idea of natural law also inspires his model for moral action.

Let us return to Kant's life. In 1755, now aged 31, Kant came back to Königsberg, gave public lectures, presented his written work to the university, published an impressive amount of his writings, received his doctorate, and consequently received authorization to work as a private teacher, a *Privatdozent*, unsalaried. This allowed him to make a living from the students who paid their fees per lecture. Kant's lecturing duties were time-and-energy consuming, and kept him busy, financially challenged, and in a bit of a purgatory for the next several years. Often motivated by student demand, he taught a variety of courses, such as anthropology, logic, mechanics, metaphysics, moral philosophy, physical geography, physics and mathematics (arithmetic, geometry, trigonometry).

It took Kant 15 years to secure a salaried position as a professor at the university, which he finally achieved in 1770, having had in the meantime to take up a supplementary position as a librarian. It is not as if he was unsuccessful or disrespected: he received offers of professorships of philosophy in other cities, and was popular as a teacher. Kant was simply not interested in leaving Königsberg, where he had established himself socially, and where he had a keen eye on a professorship in philosophy. He thus proceeded patiently.

In 1770 Kant gave his Inaugural Lecture as a new professor, and in light of his history of impressively productive scholarship, it is easy to imagine that he would have continued writing and publishing as before. What happened, though, is that Kant began to rework his ideas very quietly over the next eleven years, without having any work go into print. The result was the epoch-making work with which we will begin the study of his philosophy, the *Critique of Pure Reason*, published in 1781, which he revised for a second edition in 1787.

Kant's main preoccupation is with understanding the relationship between science and morality. This interest did not radically change, but his approach to resolving the tension between the two eventually assumed a more dramatic form. As historians of Kant's philosophical development describe it, the *Critique of Pure Reason* marks the beginning of a second major period in Kant's writings, called the 'critical' period, which contrasts with the 'pre-critical' period of his predominantly scientific writings. In his efforts to reconcile natural science – understood as a thoroughly mechanical vision of the world, potentially atheistic and amoral – with human freedom, morality and theism, Kant became critical of our ability to know anything determinate about metaphysical truth, or, in other words, the way things are in themselves. We will see exactly why in later chapters.

As occurs with many historically influential works, the *Critique of Pure Reason* was at first neither well understood nor appreciated for the groundbreaking work that it was. Within two years of its publication, Kant accordingly composed a shorter, more accessible rendition of the work, entitled *Prolegomena to any Future Metaphysics that Will be Able to Come Forward as a Science* (1783). The title suggests to everyone, one could say, to 'please read this book (and the *Critique of Pure Reason*) before engaging in traditional metaphysical speculation'.

Kant enthusiastically conceived of his *Critique* as a work with a mission: it was a peacemaking effort, trying to end once and for all, the wars among those who believed that they held, either as philosophic or religious texts, the true metaphysics, whether it happened to be theist, atheist or neutral. His position – argued at impressively detailed length – is that answers to ultimate questions are forever beyond human reach, and that philosophical and religious wars are therefore idle.

Spotlight: Kant's Copernican Revolution

Kant describes his work in the *Critique of Pure Reason* as a 'Copernican Revolution' in philosophy, comparing his philosophy to how Nicolaus Copernicus (1473–1543) revolutionized our understanding of the solar system by replacing a commonly believed 'geocentric' (earth-centred) model with an alternative 'heliocentric' (sun-centred) model: 'finding that he could not make sufficient progress by assuming that all the heavenly bodies revolved round the spectator, he thought that he might have better success by reversing the process, and having the spectator revolve, while the stars remained at rest' (Bxvi). Celestial objects may look as if they are moving of their own accord, but we are the ones who are moving, spinning around on a carousel, so to speak. The object's shifting appearance is a reflection of our own activity.

Similarly, it is still commonly believed the ordinary objects that we perceive as, for instance, being brown, square and 15 feet away, appear as such because that is part of their intrinsic and objective character. Kant's idea, however, is that an object's being brown, square and 15 feet away, is primarily due to our own mental movement, or mental contribution to the situation. Here again, the object's appearance is a reflection of our own activity.

After the publication of the *Critique of Pure Reason*, Kant's productiveness returned to its earlier, pre-critical period levels. Two years after the *Prolegomena* appeared, he published the *Groundwork of the Metaphysics of Morals* (1785), and within another two years, a revision of the *Critique* for a second edition. A year later, he published a 'second' critique, the *Critique of Practical Reason* (1788), enhancing and systematizing his work on morality. Two years later, he set forth a 'third' critique on aesthetics and purposes inherent in nature, the *Critique of the Power of Judgement* (1790).

At this point, Kant was 66 years old, maintaining his health by living intelligently and temperately according to a strict schedule that included a daily walk in the late afternoon for exercise. He continued teaching for another six years until 1796, when he retired. At age 69 he published *Religion Within the Bounds of Reason Alone* (1793), which had the effect of turning the government censorship office against him. The book was judged to be insufficiently respectful of Christianity and Kant received a written warning not to publish further on religious subjects. Frederick the Great, who had died a decade before, had left the throne to his less tolerant nephew, Frederick William II, whose ministers were then in charge of censorship. When Frederick William II died in 1797, Kant published in the same year *The Metaphysics of Morals*, which completed his moral theory, and 1798, his final two works, *Anthropology from a Pragmatic Point of View*, and *The Conflict of the Faculties*.

With his mental abilities slowly fading, Kant lived another six years, until he passed away on 12 February 1804 at the age of 79. When Kant died, the world was already moving into a new age. In that year, Napoleon Bonaparte was crowned Emperor of France, and Thomas Jefferson was elected President of the United States for a second term. Abraham Lincoln would be born exactly five years later to the day, in 1809.

Dig Deeper

Ernst Cassirer, *Kant's Life and Thought,* tr. James Haden (Yale University Press, 1981)

Arsenij Gulya, *Immanuel Kant and His Life and Thought,* tr. M. Despalatovic (Boston: Birkhauser, 1987)

Manfred Kuehn, *Kant: A Biography* (Cambridge University Press, 2001)

J. H. W. Stuckenberg, *The Life of Immanuel Kant* (London: Macmillan, 1882)

Study questions

1 What is Pietism, and what role did it play in Kant's life?

2 What were the main subjects Kant studied as a high school student? Why did these studies become important in Kant's later life as a professor?

3 Why is scientific thinking, and especially Newtonian physics and astronomy, important for understanding Kant's philosophy?

4 What is the nebular hypothesis? Was Kant the first person to formulate this hypothesis?

5 What was Kant's view on the devastating Lisbon earthquake of 1755?

6 What is the difference between Kant's 'critical' period and his 'pre-critical' period?

7 What are the titles and respective subject matters of Kant's three *Critiques*?

8 The main question in Kant's philosophy concerns reconciling the tension between which two disciplines?

9 In what sense is Kant's central work, the *Critique of Pure Reason*, an effort at peacemaking?

10 Did the government censors ever condemn any of Kant's books?

2

Kant's way of thinking and arguing

In this chapter, we will see how Kant's philosophizing rests squarely upon the discipline of Aristotelian logic and the assumption that humans are essentially rational beings. We will also see how he analyses ordinary objects into a set of fundamental dimensions – spatio-temporal, sensory and conceptual – and how he reveals the underlying presuppositions for any given subject by asking the probing question, *How is it possible?*

1 Aristotelian logic and the elementary judgement, *S is P*

When composing a philosophy, it is natural to search for a reliable foundation upon which to build it. The stronger the foundation, the better the result will be. A reason for seeking a solid foundation concerns a certain feature of truth, which is that truth is linked with *stability*. It has been traditionally and naturally thought that the more permanent something is, the truer it is. Truth is something one can hold on to, and it makes more sense to hold on to a rock, than to a puff of smoke.

The great philosopher, Plato, appreciated this feature of truth, and having noticed that even rocks crumble away, he imagined a truer dimension beyond space and time that does not fade, and that is absolutely unchanging. This realm simply 'is' – it is the realm of 'Being' – and it never 'becomes' anything different. Many people would locate God – a being that the Bible records as having said appropriately to Moses, 'I am that I am' – in this otherworldly realm of truth.

Now although Kant was a theist, he was not exactly a follower of Plato. He nonetheless took from Plato an idea to ground his philosophy. This is the thought that in contrast to physical things which change, concepts are more stable and more reliable, and hence more true – or at least certain concepts are.

Consider how one can draw a set of circles in the sand along the seashore and watch these circles wash away in minutes. Contrast how the geometrical definition of a circle – the set of points on a given flat surface that are equidistant from a given point – *does not change at all*. The definition has been there for eternity. In Plato's mind, the definition of a circle is thereby more true than any physical circle that exists in space and time. Plato held the *concept* of a circle to be truer than any particular circle that one might perceive here or there, whether it is in the shape of a full moon, a dish, or the wheel of a bicycle. This idea that certain concepts are more basic than – one could even say 'prior to' – physical things will help us understand Kant.

> **Key idea:** Truth as stability:
>
> We rely on what is true, and insofar as we rely upon it, we assume that truth is stable. Absolute truth would consequently be totally reliable and completely secure, and as such, it would be unchanging. Kant searches for the truth of human knowledge, and discovers it in the fixed forms of our mental structure.

Plato, along with his magnificent student, Aristotle, lived at a time and in a city with a long heritage of legal debate. Many talented lawyers lived in ancient Athens, and it was common to hear them argue over this or that case in the public forum, or agora, where the seat of government and law courts were located. When these lawyers argued a case, they had a variety of winning techniques at their disposal – they could, for instance, appeal to the jury's emotions or they could impress them with the established authority of their witnesses – but the ability to think logically was at the centre of their discipline.

We owe it to Aristotle's genius for having showed us exactly how and why arguments can 'sound right', even though their contents can be false or silly. One could say the following, which although odd, still rings logically true:

1 All cats are good singers.

2 All good singers have sharp teeth.

3 *Therefore*, all cats have sharp teeth.

Similarly, one could argue:

1 If moo, then doo.

2 If doo then goo.

3 *Therefore*, if moo, then goo.

Here is another example, where the contents are all true:

1 Immanuel Kant is a human being.

2 All human beings have a sense of humour.

3 *Therefore*, Immanuel Kant has a sense of humour.

The logical sequences in these examples 'sound right' for a reason that has nothing to do with the truth or falsity of what is being asserted. They sound right because the *forms* of the sequences make sense. If the premises happen to be true, then a true conclusion automatically follows. The forms are valid because they are 'truth preserving', one could say.

To display these logical forms more clearly, Aristotle substituted for the conceptual contents, merely letters that can stand for any subject matter at all. The above three arguments accordingly transform into:

1 All As are Bs.

2 All Bs have P.

3 *Therefore*, all As have P.

1 If A, then B.

2 If B, then C.

3 *Therefore*, if A, then C.

1 S is a T.

2 All Ts have P.

3 *Therefore*, S has P.

Aristotle discovered and developed the idea of displaying an argument's logical form, and he wrote at great length about various kinds of argument forms, setting out their different structures in detail. His logical studies have become central to philosophy ever since.

Now in Kant's time, Aristotelian logic was respected as a better-than-rock-solid subject. This is why Kant based his philosophy on Aristotelian logic, stating the following in the preface to the second edition (1787) of his *Critique of Pure Reason*:

> *... since* Aristotle, *logic has not had to retrace a single step, unless we choose to consider as improvements the removal of some unnecessary subtleties, or the clearer definition of its matter, both of which refer to the elegance rather than to the solidity of the science. It is remarkable also, that to the present day, it has not been able to make one step in advance, so that, to all appearance, it may be considered as completed and perfect.*
>
> (Bviii)

The logical foundations of Kant's philosophy are in fact less complicated than the examples above. They are simple, because Kant wants to identify the elementary bits of knowledge that we have, and he finds nothing more elementary than when we think to ourselves in daily experience, 'the sky is blue', or 'the sound is loud', or 'the table is hard'. These are basic judgements, as we merely take note that there is the blue sky, or a loud sound or a hard table.

If we express this kind of elementary judgement as a logical form, there is some *thing* (e.g., the sky, a sound, or a table) that has some *quality* (e.g., is blue, loud or hard). Using Aristotle's style, we can refer to the thing as *S* (for 'subject') and the quality as *P* (for 'property' which is another word for 'quality').

At the foundation of our knowledge, then, and at the foundation of Kant's philosophy, we have the logical form *S is P*, which is the form of an elementary judgement. *S* is the subject thought about, which usually refers to some individual, and *P* is the predicate, which usually indicates some quality or property that is ascribed to the subject.

We will say more about *S is P* when we consider how Kant develops his theory of knowledge out of this logical structure in the *Critique of Pure Reason*. He will introduce his own terminology, and refer to *S* as 'intuitions' and to *P* as 'concepts'. The core ideas will remain the same, though, as we are describing them here.

Spotlight: Gottlob Frege and mathematical logic

Kant's philosophy is grounded in traditional Aristotelian logic, where, as noted, the basic structure is *S is P*. Here, *S* represents some subject and *P* represents some predicate, as in *The table is green*. Aristotle also uses the words, "all," "some," and "none" to generate statements such as *All S's are P*, *Some S's are P*, *No S's are P*, as well as *All S's are not P*, and so on. In Kant's view, this way of understanding logic remained constant for a couple of thousand years, until the 19th century.

Gottlob Frege (1848–1925) reconceptualized the logical structure of sentences with a more mathematical style, revising for example, *All S's are P* (e.g., *All tables are green*) to read, *For all x's, if x is an S, then x is P* (e.g., *For all x's, if x is a table, then x is green*). The sentence, *Some S's are P* would correspondingly read, *For some x, x is an S, and x is P* (e.g., *For some x, x is a table and x is green*). In mathematics-like symbols, *All S's are P* would look like $\forall x \, (Sx \rightarrow Px)$.

Unlike Aristotelian logic, this more mathematical way to symbolize logical relations can more powerfully and clearly express the inner logic of sentences such as *Everyone is taller than someone*. In this case, we would read it as, *For every x, if x is a person, then for some y, y is a person and x is taller than y*. In mathematical logic terms, it would look like: $\forall x \, (Px \rightarrow \exists y(Py \& Txy))$.

In terms of its impact in intellectual history, Frege's development of mathematical logic is on a par with Edison's successful construction of a light bulb or the Wright brothers' successful construction of an airplane. Alan Turing (1912–1954), a specialist in mathematical logic, successfully used his logical knowledge in the British effort to crack the secret German codes during World War II, making a major breakthrough that helped the Allied forces win the war.

2 Abstraction as a way of thinking

Imagine sitting on a park bench, watching a group of birds on the grass. Some of them are brown, some are black, some are speckled, some are large, some are small, some are aggressive, some are peaceful, some are chirping, some are quietly resting and some are eating. When we use the concept 'bird' to refer to them all, we overlook these differences and think of the birds together as a group, considering them to be all the same as 'birds'. To capture the thought of 'bird', we might even offer a definition: a bird is a warm-blooded animal that has feathers, lays eggs, and has wings and a beak. In the effort to comprehend all birds in a single swoop, these qualities would be part of the 'essence' of what a bird is, as we think of 'bird-ness'.

Concepts are thus a mixed bag: they have us think superficially by preventing many of the world's tiny details to come to our explicit notice, but they allow us to group individuals together effectively. Concepts are like boxes (or bags) into which we put groups of similar individuals, usually as a matter of practical convenience. The boxes themselves often fit into each other, like a set of Russian matryoshkas or 'nesting' dolls, where the largest doll, which is hollow, has enough space within it to contain the next smallest doll, also hollow, which in turn has enough space to contain a smaller doll, all the way down to the tiniest doll, which is at the centre of the cluster. So it is often with sets of concepts: material things include living things, living things include animals, animals include mammals, and mammals include humans.

If we return to our group of birds on the grass, we can say that some styles of philosophizing – and Kant's is one of them – are more interested, for instance, in the concept of a 'bird', than in the specific features of any particular bird on the grass, even though some particular bird might be beautiful and interesting as an individual. If one were to develop a philosophy of 'birds', so to speak, this kind of philosophy would be formulated very generally, so that it could speak truthfully about each and every bird, no matter where or when a bird might live, no matter how it might look, and no matter what kind of bird it might be.

If we were to compose a philosophy of religion along similar lines, the same would be true. We would not be concerned with the differences between Christianity, Hinduism or Buddhism, or any other religion. The aim would be to find features that religions have equally in common. We would be searching for the 'universal' quality of religion in general – something timeless, true, and always reliable about religion.

Some theorists who have developed this line of thought have suggested that the *moral* qualities of every religion serve as the common ground. Since each religion instructs people to be good, it makes little difference what religion a person happens to believe in, if we focus exclusively on this moral essence.

With respect to human beings, Kant's philosophy adopts the same kind of attitude. He is not especially interested in the differences between people. He is concerned with what we have in common, and what is *always equally present* in each of us.

This idea that there is an 'essence' to human beings is not new. It stems from the long heritage of ancient Greek philosophy which characterizes the human being as a rational animal. For Kant, 'rational' specifically means 'logical', and so by his lights, if there is a human being, then the person will have *logic* as an essential feature. This is an important point to remember for understanding Kant.

As noted, Kant believes that *S is P* is the most basic logical form, so for Kant, if there is a human being, then the person's knowledge and experience will follow the contours of this elementary logical form. Kant argues that the world appears to us as it does (e.g., we experience a world with blue skies, loud sounds, hard tables and such), precisely because we think in terms of this elementary form of judgement. The structure comes from us.

Later on, our discussion of Kant's theory of knowledge will show how Kant appeals to an inventory of basic logical forms – he obtains a list of twelve from the logic books of his day – to identify the fundamental kinds of judgements which we use to think about the world. For the most part, they are variants of the *S is P* logical format. Kant's philosophy is based on the general idea that since we are essentially logical beings, we cannot help but create a logically structured world for ourselves.

Key idea: Identifying the essence of a group:

To achieve universal results in philosophy, it helps to attend exclusively to the qualities that a group of things equally share – the *essence* of the group – and to disregard their accidental differences in detail. If we consider humanity as a single group, disregarding the individual differences between people, as Kant does, one is in the position to write a philosophy true for all people for all time.

So far, we have been discussing the idea of abstraction, and how Kant's interests are defined not in reference to any specific people and their distinctive features, but reside in the concept of human beings in general. He abstracts away from differences between people and attends to features that everyone has in common, a central one of which is the capacity to think logically.

Kant's philosophy puts abstractive thought to use in another way, and to understand this, we can consider not a set of birds, but some single bird. Let us now think abstractly about that bird.

Using general terms to describe the situation, suppose that there is a thing in front of us which happens to be a bird, which has a particular colour and particular shape. Suppose it is a large bluebird. Kant believes that we can conceive of this thing in various ways by focusing exclusively on this or that one of its aspects. We can consider it as just a 'thing', for instance, and disregard its kind, its shape and its colour. Or we could attend only to the thing's shape, and disregard its colour, along with what kind of thing it happens to be. Or we could attend only to the object's kind – as we did originally when regarding the original group of birds as simply 'birds' – and disregard the object's particular shape and colour.

Being able imaginatively to separate out such features of things, holding them up individually for reflection and considering them in isolation from everything else, is a crucial feature of Kant's style of philosophizing. He grounds some of his most influential arguments on the ability to separate imaginatively, for example, a thing's shape from its colour, or a thing's shape from any thought of what kind of thing it happens to be. Kant expands this way of thinking to the point where he asserts that at bottom, our experience divides into three fundamental aspects: (1) shapes and numbers, (2) colours, tastes, sounds and other sensory qualities, and (3) concepts, which we use to understand the kinds of things we are experiencing.

When we discuss Kant's theory of space and time, his moral theory and this theory of beauty, this ability to separate one sector of experience from another will prove to be essential to understanding his arguments. The process compares well to chemical analysis, where we begin with some complicated compound or mixture, and then separate it into its component substances or elements. As a matter of philosophical theorizing, Kant similarly divides our experience into a geometrical/mathematical sector, a sensory sector and a conceptual sector, which fuse together to create our experience of the world.

3 Searching for underlying presuppositions

The idea of a 'presupposition' is easy to grasp. A presupposition is what one needs to *assume*, if something – and this 'something' could be anything at all that one wishes to consider – is to be true or is to exist. Consider the words in this sentence. For someone to read the words and understand them, we must presuppose that the person understands the English language. For someone to add a few numbers together, one must presuppose that the person knows how to count. For someone to drive a car well, one must presuppose that the person understands the difference between driving slowly and driving rapidly, and between driving on the left side of the road and driving on the right. Presuppositions determine the background context. They are the soil from which our more detailed knowledge extends.

The activity of discerning and disclosing presuppositions is different from that of drawing logical implications. Take as an example $4 = 2 + 2$. If we know that $2 = 1 + 1$, we can infer that $4 = 1 + 1 + 1 + 1$. We can draw potentially an infinite number of inferences from $4 = 2 + 2$, once it is recognized, for instance, that $1 = ¼ + ¾$ and that $1 = ¼ + ¼ + ¼ + ¼$. Such inferences could go on forever.

The process of looking for presuppositions, however, is different. With respect to disclosing presuppositions, we can ask in the case of $4 = 2 + 2$: What is required for there to be a statement such as $4 = 2 + 2$ at all? How is $4 = 2 + 2$ possible? One answer is that, to begin with, we must presuppose a mathematical system. Another is that we must assume that the meanings of the numerical symbols remain constant from one day to the next. Another would be – possibly – that there is a prior social practice called 'adding' in which people engage.

This last presupposition may seem reasonable. Suppose, however, that one believes that $4 = 2 + 2$ has been true from eternity, as might a follower of Plato. If so, then the equation would be true independently of whether there happen to be human beings who speak to each other about mathematics. For $4 = 2 + 2$ to be true, social practices might not be required.

The above example shows that the search for presuppositions can sometimes lead to uncertain or puzzling results. It also suggests – and this complicates the situation considerably – that what counts as a presupposition can depend on the philosophical commitments one has operating in the background.

Kant has a special way to describe the activity of looking for presuppositions. If we have an object in front of us such as a bird, a human, a wheel, or a mathematical statement, Kant will ask, '*How is it possible?*' for there to be a bird, or a person, or wheel, etc. The question, '*How is it possible?*' is asking for the presuppositions involved in the thing's presence. In the case of the bird, an answer would be: *for a bird to be in front of us*, we must presuppose a spatial location for the bird to be in. We must also presuppose a time in which we can experience the bird. These are broad and basic presuppositions, exactly of the kind that Kant's philosophy aims to disclose.

A simple way to express this quest for presuppositions is in the following form of argument:

Question: 'How is P possible?'

1 We know that P.

2 If Q were false, then P would be false.

3 So Q must be true.

Using our bird example above, we could say:

1 We know that there is a bird in front of us.

2 If there were no space for the bird to be in, then there could be no bird in front of us.

3 So there must be space for the bird to be in (i.e., we must 'presuppose' the presence of space to begin with, for there to be an experience of a bird).

This style of argumentation can sometimes go wrong. Consider the following:

1 We know that the glass is filled with water.

2 If it were false that someone had filled the glass with water, then there would be no water in the glass.

3 So, someone filled the glass with water.

The problem is in the second step. There are other ways in which the glass might have become filled with water. Perhaps the water came from a leak in the ceiling.

In the other example above, where it is argued that we need to presuppose space in order to perceive a bird, one might question the argument – again, in the second step – by asserting that a 'bird' is really nothing more than a collection of ideas in my mind. Since there is no 'space' in my mind, there is no need to presuppose space for the 'bird' to be in. The upshot is that one should always adopt a cautious attitude towards arguments that claim to reveal and establish presuppositions, because they can sometimes go wrong, despite looking very reasonable. Kant often uses such arguments.

To conclude and summarize, we can observe that Kant's way of thinking and arguing has a number of key features:

1 Kant assumes that Aristotelian logic is fundamental to human thought and being, and that among the various logical forms, *S is P* is the most basic.

2 Kant assumes that human beings are essentially *logical* beings who think necessarily in terms of logical forms.

3 Kant separates the generic features of physical objects into three basic kinds, namely, 'concepts', 'shapes/numbers' and 'sensations'.

4 Kant tries to disclose underlying presuppositions for our experience by using questions such as '*how is it possible that...?*'

Study questions

1 According to Plato, which item would best reflect the nature of truth: (1) a passing cloud, (2) an apple, (3) a human body, (4) a rock? Why? Does Plato believe that there is anything truer than these items?

2 Do you believe that the geometrical definition of a circle had been true (or similarly, equations such as *2 + 2 = 4*) long before human beings came onto the earthly scene? Why or why not?

3 Using letters (e.g., as in *All T's have P*, as above), how would one write out the logical form of the following argument: 'All cats have four legs, all dogs have four legs, and therefore all cats are dogs'. Is this a valid form of argument?

4 Why does Kant build his philosophy upon the logical form, *S is P*?

5 Kant believes that humans are essentially rational beings. He has, however, a very specific way to understand the idea of 'rational'. What is this specific way?

6 Would you expect Kant's theory of knowledge to be sensitive to the differences between older and younger people, or between ancient and modern people, or between men and women? If not, why not?

7 A thought experiment: consider any item in your immediate surroundings, (e.g., a cup, a table, a tree, etc.) and analyse it carefully according to its shape, its colour and the kind of thing that it is.

8 What is a presupposition? How is the practice of drawing logical implications different from that of revealing presuppositions?

9 How can the activity of revealing presuppositions sometimes yield uncertain results?

10 Using the same object from question 7, now ask about the object in the Kantian style, '*How is it* (e.g., the cup, or table, etc.) *possible?*'

Section Two:

What can we know?

3

Kant's theory of knowledge

We see the blue sky, the green light, the white clouds, the red flag, and make elementary judgements. Kant identifies the abstract form of these judgements, where we apprehend some thing and ascribe a particular quality to it, as *S is P*. He then reflects upon this basic logical form to develop a theory of knowledge.

In this chapter, we will consider Kant's critique of the British empiricist understanding of the concept of causality. This critique is based on the interrelationship between two distinctions: (1) analytic judgements versus synthetic judgements, and (2) judgements known to be true *a priori* versus those known to be true *a posteriori*. Emerging from this interrelationship is Kant's famous recognition of a special kind of judgement, namely, one that is synthetic, but known also to be true *a priori*. The chapter concludes by showing how Kant used the abstract form of elementary judgements, *S is P*, to develop an account of how our mental faculties interact when we make judgements.

1 British empiricism: questioning the foundations of science

'I'll believe it when I see it.' This familiar remark recalls how first-hand personal experience is commonly accepted as a convincing way – if not the fundamental way – to determine what to believe in. Many centuries ago, for instance, it was unbelievable that there could be organisms so small as to be invisible to the naked eye. Opinions changed after microscopes allowed us to see these tiny creatures in the late 1600s.

This emphasis upon direct personal experience is philosophically expandable to the point of prescribing how words must derive their meaning. The prescription would be: if any given word is to be *meaningful*, then it must be traceable back to some sensory experience. Otherwise, the word should be regarded as only a meaningless sound. This experience-tied theory of meaning was advocated by the Scottish philosopher, David Hume (1711–1776).

This does not mean that our words must refer only to things that exist. There may be no unicorns living in the world's forests, but the word 'unicorn' is meaningful as the combination of 'horse' and 'horn' – items of which we do have direct experience. The name 'Hercules' is similarly meaningful as the enlargement of the idea of a physically strong person. The elements of our words must refer to things in actual experience, although the words themselves might not.

Hume was an empiricist philosopher, where an 'empiricist' is someone who holds that what exists or what is true in a non-trivial sense, can be known only through some observation about how the world is. To know anything, there must first be some sensory experience. The eighteenth-century British empiricists accordingly supposed that the mind is empty when experience begins, like a blank writing slate or 'tabula rasa', as the English philosopher, John Locke (1632–1704) described it. Sensory experience 'writes' upon our initially blank tablet, so to speak.

Since the empiricist outlook requires us to observe and experience the world before making any claims about what is true or what exists, one might expect it to be friendly to the scientific outlook, which also relies upon observation and experimentation. There is a surprisingly tense relationship, however, between empiricist philosophy and scientific thinking, for as we shall now see, strict empiricists have a doubtful attitude towards the concept of 'causality', upon which scientific thought is based.

At the foundation of scientific reasoning is the relationship of causality, for without this concept, it would be impossible to formulate any natural laws. We would like to say, for example, that heating water to a temperature of 100°C under standard conditions will cause water to boil, or that the exposure to light will cause a chemical reaction on photographic film. Without a meaningful conception of causality, we cannot defensibly make such assertions.

Let us then consider how the concept of causality derives its meaning in empiricist terms – and most importantly, what kind of meaning it has on this empiricist view – by applying the definition of linguistic meaning mentioned above. Now science requires a concept of causality which expresses the thought that two events are *necessarily* linked. We cannot assert that water boils at 100° C and allow that under the exact same environmental conditions, it could boil one day at 100°, another day at 110°, and yet another day at 90°. If we assert that water boils at 100° C, we intend that water *necessarily* boils at that temperature, given how the world physically and constantly is. The claim about water's boiling point predicts the future, which is what science is all about.

The scientific way, and also the common-sense way, to understand causality is to recognize that one event *a* is linked with another event *b* through a relationship of *necessary connection*. This gives us three components to the meaning of the word 'causality': (1) event *a*, (2) event *b*, and (3) a relationship between *a* and *b* – call it *R* – that is the 'necessary connection'. We can write this in shorthand as *aRb*.

To understand the meaning of the word 'causality' in empiricist terms, we will need to experience each of these three elements individually and specify what they are. An easy test case will help, in which we can look carefully for each of these three elements in our experience. Imagine that we are watching someone bouncing a ball in a gymnasium. We see the ball hitting the floor repeatedly and we hear a 'bouncing' sound each time it hits. We naturally say that the sound is caused by the ball hitting the floor. Applying the empiricist theory of meaning, let us look for the individual experiences that correspond to the three components mentioned above, namely, the *a*, the *b* and the *R*. What do we observe?

The *a* and *b* – the ball striking the floor and the sound that follows – are perceived straightforwardly. The problem is with the *R*. The empiricist surprise is that aside from the *a* and the *b*, there is nothing objectively 'out there' on the gymnasium floor further to observe with respect to causality. We do not see the ball hitting the floor, and then observe some 'link' between the ball hitting the floor and the sound, as if there were a wire or chain connecting them together. Our direct experience of what is out there on the gymnasium floor, is of two events in succession, and only those two events. The *R* is not there.

Now there *is* an experience that corresponds to the *R* which completes the meaning of the word 'causality', but this is not the experience of an objective link that can be identified as 'necessary connection'. It is something different. To find the *R*, we need to look inward and consider our own feelings, rather than observe what is happening out there on the gymnasium floor.

The experience associated with the *R* is the *feeling of expectation* that occurs when we see the *a*. In our example, it would be the expectation that we will soon hear a sound as we watch the ball moving towards the ground. Having seen many bouncing balls in the past, the expectation is a matter of custom or habit. It is psychological and 'subjective'. Although it would be strange indeed, it objectively remains possible that the ball could hit the gymnasium floor and no sound would follow. Nothing precludes this. The future might not be like the past.

The unexpected result is that the meaning of 'causality' on this empiricist theory of linguistic meaning is not 'necessary connection', but 'conventional association through custom or habit'. In our past experience, events have appeared in conjunction with one another, or have been 'constantly conjoined', but they need not have been, and they need not be so conjoined in the future.

This result goes a long way towards undermining scientific inquiry. The empiricist asks that we observe the world carefully in order to ground our knowledge, and observation shows that the concept of causality upon which natural science is based, lacks the strength to make solid predictions. The only legitimate meaning for 'causality', so it appears, is psychological association' rather than 'objective and necessary connection'.

Kant found this empiricist account of causality to be *unbelievable*, convinced as he was that scientific inquiry has a stronger basis than mere habit. Rather than accepting that empiricist philosophy had established that scientific theory is objectively groundless, he assumed that the problem resides within empiricism itself. Located among the theoretical possibilities that it could not recognize, was the correct way to ground the notion of causality as necessary connection.

Key idea: Causality as 'necessary connection':

To ensure predictability between events, a scientific theory requires a concept of causality as 'necessary connection'. Kant's theory of knowledge intends to re-establish this concept by refuting David Hume's sceptical conception of causality as the expression of simply habit and custom.

How, then, does Kant question and criticize British empiricist philosophy? His criticism is implicit in our initial chapter on Kant's way of thinking. Specifically, he challenges the empiricists by casting doubt on their idea that *all* knowledge arises from sensory experience.

Kant asserts to the contrary that our minds are *not* originally like blank slates, blank pieces of paper or empty mirrors when sensory information begins to impress itself on our minds.

Although our minds may be empty of sensory content before experience begins, they nonetheless *have a prior structure* that *gives shape* to the sensory experience. We are essentially rational beings according to Kant, and so logic and rationality are in us before experience begins. These give shape to our experience.

Kant develops his challenge to empiricism in a technical way by focusing on the empiricist theory of judgement, which we will now briefly describe. Since empiricists recognize sensory experience as the exclusive way to obtain knowledge of a non-trivial sort, they hold that our fundamental knowledge-carrying statements are simple matters of fact that refer to things in the world, their qualities or their relationships. Aside from this, there are only the definitions of words that we construct. These definitions are always 'true', but they are uninformatively so, since we construct the definitions ourselves. Matters of fact, when true, are substantially true because we have observed the world to be such.

In his *An Enquiry Concerning Human Understanding* (1748), Hume accordingly divides our knowledge-related judgements into two large classes: (1) relations of ideas and (2) matters of fact. Relations of ideas include geometry, algebra and arithmetic; matters of fact include observations that the sky is blue, the grass is green, and so on. These latter bits of knowledge are available only by taking a look to see how the world is. The philosopher, Leibniz, worked with a similar distinction between truths of reason and truths of fact.

Kant's breakthrough was to ask whether the distinction between relations of ideas and matters of fact is fully comprehensive. Kant asked, because he was discerning that the distinction between relations of ideas and matters of fact was letting slip through the cracks, certain kinds of judgements that count equally as knowledge. Hume himself, who died five years before Kant published the *Critique of Pure Reason*, believed adamantly that his division was exhaustive, and he concluded his *Enquiry* with a dramatic remark to this effect. Any supposedly knowledgeable book that is not based on either relations of ideas or matters of fact, is suitable for the rubbish incinerator:

> If we take in our hand any volume; of divinity or school metaphysics, for instance; let us ask, Does it contain any abstract reasoning concerning quantity or number? No. Does it contain any experimental reasoning concerning matter of fact and existence? No. Commit it then to the flames: for it can contain nothing but sophistry and illusion.

2 Kant's theory of judgement: questioning the foundations of empiricism

In his effort to develop a theory of knowledge, Kant acknowledges the initial plausibility of Hume's distinction between relations of ideas and matters of fact. Theorizing at a deeper level, however, he starts with the *S is P* format, since both relations of ideas and matters of fact assume this form. Kant's preliminary concern is with the *S is P* logical format, where he asks us to consider the possible relationships between *S* and *P*.

There are only two options. In judgements of the form, *S is P*, either the meaning of the predicate *P* is *contained* in the meaning of the subject *S* or it is *not contained* in the meaning of the subject, and adds something new. Take the first option. If *S* is *bachelor*, then the concept *male* is contained in *S*'s meaning. The judgement, 'the bachelor is male', does little more than render a component of *S*'s meaning explicit. Judgements of this kind 'analyse' *S*, so to speak, and Kant refers to them as *analytic* judgements. They are true, but uninformative.

We should note that when saying that in analytic judgements, the predicate *P* is 'contained in' the subject *S*, it is easy to confuse what is meant by 'contained in'. Consider this question: is the concept *animal* contained in the concept *cat*, or is the concept *cat* contained in the concept *animal*? One might at first think that *cat* is contained in *animal*, since *animal* includes many varieties, such as cats, dogs, sheep, goats, and so on. This, however, is not how Kant is thinking of 'contained in'. To return to our example above, the idea would not be that *male*, contains *bachelor*, where the generic group of males contains both married and unmarried males, young and old males, and tall and short males. Kant has a different idea in mind.

The 'containment' situation compares closely to how a bowl of tomato soup always has both liquid and tomatoes. When we say 'the tomato soup has liquid' or the 'tomato soup has tomatoes', we render explicit the components of the concept *tomato soup*. We learn nothing new. Similarly, we could analyse the component parts of the concept *triangle*, and say, 'the triangle has three sides'. In these examples, the idea of 'containment in' involves starting with a relatively rich concept – one that contains a number of components which together define the concept. The analytic judgements that express the contents of that richer concept, make explicit this or that aspect of the concept's meaning.

Such is Kant's understanding of analytic judgements, where the meaning of the predicate is contained in the meaning of the subject. Analytic judgements are consequently *uninformative*, since they only render explicitly what we already know implicitly. Aside from geometry, algebra and mathematics, which Kant will interpret differently, Hume's class of relations of ideas corresponds to Kant's class of analytic judgements.

We can turn now to the second option. This is when the meaning of the predicate is *not* contained in the meaning of the subject. Kant refers to these as 'synthetic' judgements, since the predicate adds new information that is not implicit in the subject. Unlike analytic judgements, all synthetic judgements are informative.

It seems that as of yet, Kant does not appear to have criticized or significantly modified Hume's distinction between relations of ideas and matters of fact, since it appears that he has only expressed Hume's distinction with a new terminology. It seems that Kant is simply using *S is P* as the basis of his account, along with the idea of predicates as either contained or not contained in the subject.

The innovative aspect of Kant's theory of judgement involves a second distinction, which when superimposed upon the analytic/synthetic distinction, yields some startling implications. The analytic/synthetic distinction essentially concerns whether or not a given judgement is informative. This second distinction concerns the different ways to determine whether or not a given judgement is true.

For any judgement, *S is P*, there will be items to which the judgement refers. Our new question is whether we need to examine those items to determine whether or not *S is P* is true. If *S is P* were 'this bachelor is unmarried', for example, and supposing the person referred to is a bachelor, it would be senseless to say to the person, 'Excuse me, I heard that you are a bachelor, so I'd like ask whether you happen to be unmarried'.

Once we know that a person is a bachelor, we know prior to meeting the person that he is unmarried.

If a man is a bachelor, we know *a priori*, as Kant would say, that the man is unmarried. Moreover, if a man is a bachelor, it is *necessarily true* that he is unmarried. *Every* such man is unmarried. So if we can know a judgement to be true without having to experience the items to which the judgement refers – if we can know a judgement to be true *before* experiencing the items to which the judgement refers – we know the judgement to be true *a priori*.

According to Kant, all *a priori* knowledge is necessary and universal. Every bachelor is necessarily unmarried and there are no exceptions. From the standpoint of philosophical propositions, it would be good to have some propositions in our theory that are known *a priori*, since these would be necessarily true and would apply universally.

In contrast, when we must experience the items to which the *S is P* judgement refers to know whether or not it is true, we are dealing with contingent matters of fact. Any one of them could be otherwise. If we were to assert, for instance, 'This bachelor is 24 years old', we would need to know something about the bachelor's history to know whether the statement is true. Such judgements are known to be true (or false) only 'after' examining the items to which the judgement refers. Kant refers to knowledge gained by this kind of examination, knowledge *a posteriori*.

If we combine our two distinctions, (a) the analytic/synthetic distinction, and (b) the *a priori/a posteriori* distinction, some valuable results emerge that go far beyond Hume's distinction between relations of ideas and matters of fact.

We can begin by drawing one obvious conclusion which concerns analytic judgements. If all analytic judgements are true simply by virtue of the meanings of their words, then to determine their truth, it is not necessary to examine the items to which the judgements refer. All analytic judgements are thus known *a priori*.

Suppose we defined a judgement where the subject already contains the predicate, but that to determine whether the judgement is true, one nonetheless had to examine the items in the world to which the judgement refers. This would be contradictory, for if the subject contains the predicate, we already know that the judgement is true. So there are no analytic judgements that are true *a posteriori*.

Among synthetic judgements, where the predicate is not contained in the subject, there are many whose truth can be determined only by examining the items to which the judgement refers. If we say, 'the cat is large', deciding whether the judgement is true involves examining the cat. Some synthetic judgements are thus known *a posteriori*, and perhaps the majority of them are known in this way. Hume's view is that they are all known *a posteriori*, since his view entails that all synthetic judgements are matters of fact.

This is exactly where Kant disagrees with Hume. Kant wonders whether there are any judgements that are informative – that is, synthetic – which are nonetheless necessarily true – that is, known *a priori*. He consequently poses this question: 'Are there any synthetic *a priori* judgements?' It is a crucial and philosophically groundbreaking question, and Kant's answer is positive. If one can identify any judgements of this sort, they would establish a solid and outstanding ground for one's philosophy. *Informative* judgements that are *necessarily true* would tell us much, either about ourselves or about the world.

We will say more about synthetic *a priori* judgements – in particular mathematical and geometrical judgements – when we consider Kant's theory of space and time. The examples of mathematical and geometrical judgements that Kant offers are controversial, however, and it is difficult to appreciate from them the strength and importance of synthetic *a priori* judgements. We will use an alternative and more straightforward example of a synthetic *a priori* judgement which Kant also mentions. It is 'all events are caused'.

Contrast these two judgements: (1) 'all *effects* are caused' and (2) 'all *events* are caused'. The first is analytic and is true *a priori*, merely by virtue of the meanings of the words. By definition, to be an 'effect *is* nothing other than to be caused'.

The statement is necessarily true, but it is also trivially true. It is an analytic *a priori* judgement.

Now the judgement, 'all events are caused' is another matter. This judgement is thought-provoking. To be an 'event' does not logically entail being 'caused', for although it is remote and virtually unimaginable, it is not contradictory to assert that something could happen spontaneously, 'out of nowhere'. For Kantian reasons that we will later see, every human being has a difficult time imagining this. Nonetheless, admitting the mere possibility of an 'uncaused event' is not the same as proposing an idea like 'round square', 'wooden iron', or 'reddish green'. The idea of 'uncaused effect' may be a contradiction, but that of an 'uncaused event' is not.

This is to say that 'all events are caused' is a synthetic judgement where the predicate is not contained in the subject. We learn something new through it. In fact, the judgement makes a strong philosophical claim, asserting that determinism is true. Kant adds importantly that there is a sense in which 'all events are caused' is *necessarily* true: it is necessary, he maintains, relative to how we need to think about the world as rational human beings, as he will later argue.

This is why in our example above, it is so difficult to imagine an uncaused event. The thought goes against our rational grain. So here, then, is a prime example of a synthetic *a priori* judgement. If there is a human being, then we know beforehand, without examining how the world is, that the person will think scientifically and will regard every event as having a cause.

We can summarize Kant's theory of judgement in the following chart:

	A priori	A posteriori
Analytic	'All effects are caused'	–
	'The cat is an animal'	
	'Bachelors are unmarried'	
Synthetic	'All events are caused'	'This effect is loud'
	'5 + 7 = 12'	'This event is profound'
		'The cat is brown'

3 Intuitions and concepts

Now that we have described Kant's theory of judgement with its various kinds of *S is P* type judgements, we can look at judgements from a new angle. This is from the standpoint of *what happens in our minds* when we make a judgement of the form *S is P*.

At one level, Kant's conception of this mental activity is straightforward. First, working with the *S is P* format, he begins by considering our ideas of the *S*'s. The *S*'s are individuals, and Kant refers to our awareness of individuals as 'intuitions'. The German word translated here into English as 'intuition' is *Anschauung*, which is worth dwelling upon for a moment.

In German, the verb *schauen* means 'to look', and the prefix *an* means 'at'. The verb *anschauen* means 'to look at'. So the term *Anschauung* means 'a-looking-at' or a 'view'. An associated term *Weltanschauung* means 'world-view' or world-outlook'. This all conveys the idea that typically, an 'intuition' refers to our direct perception of an ordinary individual thing, such as a table, chair, cup, window, car, or tree.

Second, Kant considers our ideas of the *P*'s. These are predicates or general properties that we ascribe to individuals. Kant refers to them as 'concepts', which is the translation of the German word *Begriff*. This is also an informative word to examine. It is related to the verb *greifen*, which means 'to hold' or 'to grasp'. The underlying thought is that a concept 'holds things together' and allows us to 'comprehend' a set of things in one grasp. We see this in the word 'comprehend' which literally means 'hold together'. Another related word – an important one for Kant, as we shall see – is 'synthesis' which also means to hold together. So when we think of our ideas of the Ps, we have predicates, concepts, comprehension, synthesis, and grasping, all tied together linguistically in the idea of a concept.

At the level of actual thinking processes when we 'know' something, the format *S is P* indicates a mental fusion of *intuitions* (the *S*'s) with *concepts* (the *P*'s). Just as the form of judgement *S is P* involves a unity of two different kinds of grammatical or logical elements, neither of which constitutes a judgement when taken individually, Kant maintains that intuitions and concepts are also two different kinds of elements in our awareness, neither of which alone provides knowledge. For there to be crisp, determinate knowledge of the world around us, an individual must be presented to our consciousness, and *then* a concept must be applied to that individual, or intuition, so that we can identify the kind of thing we are perceiving.

When Kant considers how the mind must work in order to apply concepts to given individuals for the sake of obtaining knowledge of the world, he creates a psychological model that mirrors the *S is P* format. Using the logical format as his guide, and having associated intuitions with the *S*'s and concepts with the *P*'s, he hypothesizes that there is a section of the mind – a 'faculty' – that apprehends the individuals and 'presents' them to consciousness, and another section of the mind that contains our concepts, and which harmonizes with the individual-presenting section, thus allowing us to apply a concept to the given individual.

In other words, Kant supposes that there is a compartment of the mind that contains the *S*'s and another, complementary compartment of the mind that contains the *P*'s. Just as *S and P* are combined in a judgement, the two mental faculties operate together: the faculty that presents and contains the *S*'s combines with the faculty that contains and applies the *P*'s to the *S*'s.

From the elementary structure of judgement, Kant thus derives a theory of how the mind works when it knows things. He first refers to intuitions and concepts that correspond the *S's* and the *P's* and which combine in our minds when we make a judgement, and then he refers to two sections of the mind that contain respectively, the intuitions and the concepts, and which themselves interact harmoniously to allow intuitions and concepts to be brought together.

Kant refers to the faculty that presents individuals to consciousness as 'sensibility' and the faculty that applies concepts to the presented individuals as 'understanding'. Parallel to and structurally matching the *S is P* interrelationship at the 'theory of knowledge' level, we have the interaction between the two cognitive faculties of sensibility and knowledge, which are both equally valued and interdependent. Kant describes this situation in the following excerpt from the *Critique of Pure Reason*:

> *Neither of these qualities or faculties is preferable to the other. Without sensibility, objects would not be given to us, and without understanding, they would not be thought by us. Thoughts without content are empty, intuitions without concepts are blind. Therefore it is equally necessary to make our concepts sensuous, i.e., to add to them their object in intuition, as to make our intuitions intelligible, that is, bring them under concepts. These two powers or faculties cannot exchange their functions. The understanding can intuit nothing, the senses can think nothing.*
> (A51/B75)

We can now describe the more detailed structures of the faculty of sensibility and the faculty of understanding. The faculty of sensibility will be structured according to the forms of space and time. The faculty of understanding will be structured according to a set of basic logical forms. After describing the respective structures of these two faculties, we will work through Kant's explanation of how the understanding's logical structure combines with the sensibility's spatio-temporal structure. This is a challenging task for Kant, since he comes to realize that aside from their similarities, the understanding and the sensibility have some strong differences to overcome, if they are to be brought into harmony.

Following Kant's sequence of exposition in the *Critique of Pure Reason*, and also following the path of an object that is given to us in experience, to which we subsequently apply a concept to say what kind of thing it is, we will first consider the structure of sensibility, and second, the structure of the understanding. This brings us to the subject of our next chapter: Kant's theories of space and time, which he describes as "forms" of sensibility that we can know *a priori*.

Dig Deeper

Henry Allison, *Custom and Reason in Hume: A Kantian Reading of the First Book of the Treatise* (Oxford University Press, 2008)

Tom Beauchamp and Alexander Rosenberg, *Hume and the Problem of Causation* (Oxford University Press, 1981)

Paul Guyer, Knowledge, *Reason and Taste: Kant's Response to Hume* (Princeton University Press, 2008)

Wayne M. Martin, *Theories of Judgement: Psychology, Logic, Phenomenology* (Cambridge University Press, 2006)

Eric Watkins, *Kant and the Metaphysics of Causality* (Cambridge University Press, 2005)

Study questions

1 How would you define 'empiricism'? In a sentence, how would you state the empiricist theory of linguistic meaning?

2 Using the empiricist theory of linguistic meaning, how would you explain the meaning of the words 'sphinx' and 'God'?

3 Using the empiricist theory of linguistic meaning, how would you explain the meaning of the word 'causality'? Why might this present a problem for the foundations of scientific thinking?

4 What did Kant think of the empiricist conception of causality?

5 Briefly characterize Hume's distinction between 'relations of ideas' and 'matters of fact'. How well does this fit with Kant's distinctions between 'analytic' and 'synthetic' judgements?

6 How does Kant use the *S is P* format to distinguish between (1) analytic and synthetic judgements, (2) intuitions and concepts, and (3) sensibility and understanding?

7 What are the two main characteristics of *a priori* knowledge?

8 Why are synthetic *a priori* judgements philosophically valuable? Why is 'all events are caused' a synthetic *a priori* judgement?

9 What is the difference between an 'intuition' and a 'concept'?

10 What two faculties must be in harmony when we make a judgement that combines an intuition and a concept?

4

Space and time: the structure of the faculty of sensibility

Among the most influential arguments in Kant's philosophy are those which conclude that space and time are, as far as we can know, nothing more than features of the human mind which organize sensory inputs. This chapter will consider these arguments, and explain how they answer the crucial Kantian question, 'How are synthetic *a priori* judgements possible?' We will also describe some developments in the study of geometry after Kant's death which, for some, cast contemporary doubt upon Kant's position.

1 Newton and Leibniz on space and time

Space is like ourselves: although we live with ourselves constantly and with great familiarity, when we ask who or what we essentially are, the question usually leaves us dumbfounded. How a condition so close to us can be so inexplicable, is the puzzle surrounding space as well. To unveil space's deepest truth, one might imagine travelling to the far corners of the universe, but no matter how far one travels, resolving that mystery is no different from fathoming the distance between one's eyes and the words on this page.

Writing over 1500 years ago in his *Confessions*, St. Augustine felt the same way about time: 'What then is time? If no one asks me, I know: if I wish to explain it to one that asks, I know not...' (Book XI). For some thinkers and for most people, space and time are as real as can be; for others, they are illusions on a cosmic scale. For Kant, space and time reside between these extremes.

To appreciate Kant's comprehension of space and time, it helps to understand the accounts against which he was reacting, namely, those of Isaac Newton (1642–1727) and Newton's contemporary, Gottfried Wilhelm Leibniz (1646–1716). Although expressing diametrically opposed views on the nature of space and time, it is a historical curiosity that during the late 1600s, Newton and Leibniz discovered calculus as a mathematical method within years of each other.

Newton regarded space and time as realities independent of the human mind: there is an absolute, immovable and inflexible space within which all locations are originally plotted, and an absolute, uniformly moving time within which all movements take place. Both space and time are empty containers, existing prior to all material content, so he believed.

Although Kant realized its usefulness for scientific studies – a usefulness he hoped to preserve within his own view – he saw Newton's theory of absolute space and time as threatening to morality and human freedom. If space and time are absolute, then mathematical, geometrical and causal relationships would apply within the universe absolutely. Our world would be a single, predictable, mechanical world, devoid of freedom.

Moreover, if space and time are absolute, and if one believes in God, then space and time would have to be among God's features. The spatio-temporal world, with all of the imperfection and pain it contains, would then be either wholly or partially equated with God himself – a pantheistic proposition which at the time, was sounding more like atheism than theism. Kant rejected this equation in favour of a more traditional conception, where God is set beyond and independent of time and space. He consequently sought a way to conceive of time and space that would preserve their scientific effectiveness, but which would keep space and time separated from the absolute order of things. His way to do this, as we shall see, was to conceive of them as being merely modes of human awareness.

Contrasting with Newton's more natural conception of space and time, Leibniz's account makes sense only in reference to his extraordinary metaphysical outlook, inspired by his work in mathematics. According to Leibniz, the universe is composed of a set of simple substances, where each substance is an independent soul with a set of God-given perceptions. The souls are not located in space or time. Time and space are only the orderings of the respective perceptions within each of these spiritual points.

Neither do the simple souls interact with each other. Each is an isolated, self-enclosed, 'windowless' whole. Each soul's set of perceptions is nonetheless synchronized with all of the others, like an arrangement of movie theatres along a street, all of which play a similar movie, and where each movie contains a segment that represents what is happening simultaneously in the other movies. God, as the supreme soul and centrally controlling movie projectionist, one could say, coordinates this set of souls in a pre-established harmony. Another name for simple soul is 'monad', which Leibniz uses to characterize these substances, or fundamental spiritual points that constitute the universe.

To imagine Leibniz's view of space (and by analogy, of time), consider two blindfolded people playing chess against each other using only verbal communication, each of whom has in mind an image of the chessboard upon which they are playing. No 'real' chessboard exists in an objective, external space independently of their imaginations, but there is a meaningful coordination between the two chessboard pictures that each imaginatively constructs.

Since each simple soul has a set of perceptions, or 'objects' as its contents, space and time become nothing more than sets of relationships between these perceptions or objects. On Leibniz's view, the souls and their objects come first, and space and time appear as secondary structures derived in reference to the perceptual contents of the simple souls. Within this outlook, space and time are merely relationships, or orderings, between perceived objects, so without supposing some objects with which to start (i.e., without some initial, God-given perceptual contents of the simple souls), there would be no space or time.

On this particular point, Kant disagrees. He maintains that the objects in space and time cannot exist independently of space and time. To him, the reverse is true: first, we have in our minds the empty containers of space and time, and then, our sensory experience fills space and time with objects that it gives to us.

Leibniz argues furthermore, though, that since God does not need space and time to perceive things, space and time cannot be absolute beings. He also notes that God would have no reason to construct a world in either a predominantly left-handed or predominantly right-handed way, so left-handedness and right-handedness must also be illusory. His views on space and time are unconventional, but Leibniz does have some challenging arguments to support it.

Kant's view is that since we cannot know whether or not God exists to begin with, it is difficult to say whether there are any perceptions that are independent of space and time in the universe. He also observes that we cannot translate a left-hand glove into a right-hand glove – these are incongruent counterparts – so any conception of space needs to recognize the reality of left-handedness and right-handedness, and hence, must recognize a more 'objective' conception of space and time than that Leibniz proposed.

2 Kant: space and time as *a priori* intuitions

Kant offers a series of arguments which establish an intermediary position between Newton and Leibniz. Unlike Newton's conception of absolute space, Kant maintains that as far as we can know, space and time are only functions of the human mind that give order to our perceptions. Unlike Leibniz, Kant recognizes that space and time must be prior to the objects that are contained in them, thus lending space and time a reality that is independent of their material contents.

Kant initially points out that space and time are not concepts, but are individualistic entities. He observes that when we refer to space and time, we think of them as 'wholes' that have 'parts'. The many parts of space constitute the entirety of space, and the many parts, or moments, of time constitute the infinity of time.

This whole/part relationship is of a different order from the relationships that hold between a concept and its instances. Consider the concept of 'blue' or 'blueness'. There are many blue things in the world, but we do not conceive of each instance of blueness literally as a part of some endless, cosmic sheet of blue, as if this sheet had been cut into parts with a scissor and pasted onto objects to make them look blue. Neither do we conceive of blue as a large pot of paint in a world beyond which it diminishes in volume as the number of blue objects in the world increases.

The relationship between a concept and its instances is different in kind from the relationship between a whole and its parts. Note how the concept of blue would stay the same, even if all of the blue items in the world disappeared. This is not true about the parts of space or time. Were all of the parts of space or time to disappear, so would space and time themselves. Kant consequently denies that space and time are concepts, and refers to them instead as 'intuitions', that is, as individuals.

Key idea: Space and time are intuitions, not concepts:

Kant maintains that space and time are wholes composed of parts. As such, they are *individuals*, associated with the faculty of *sensibility*, rather than being generalized abstractions which issue from the faculty of understanding.

The intuitions of space and time, Kant claims furthermore, are only formal structures, and are knowable *a priori*. To understand this, we need to recall his theory of knowledge. We have seen how the most elementary form of our knowledge can be expressed abstractly as the judgement S is P, where S is an individual and P is a concept. Since individuals are different in kind from concepts, to account for the possibility of such judgements, Kant postulates two distinct areas or 'faculties' within the mind that interact, as described in the previous chapter. One faculty, 'sensibility', contains the intuitions, and another faculty, 'understanding', contains the concepts. For there to be any knowledge of the form S is P, these two faculties must interact harmoniously, so that sensibility can supply the S's and understanding can supply the P's to form judgements. When we discuss Kant's aesthetic theory, we will revisit this idea of two faculties working together in harmony to produce judgements.

As mentioned, Kant does not believe with the British empiricists that the mind is totally blank at first. His view is that a human being has the faculties of sensibility and understanding from the start, and that each faculty has its own particular structure, knowable *a priori*. The structure is there in the mind before any experience occurs, present initially to give order to the incoming sensations. Now with regard to the faculty of sensibility, Kant reasons as follows:

> *It is clear that it cannot be sensation again through which sensations are arranged and placed in certain forms. Therefore, although the matter of all phenomena is given us a posteriori, their form must be ready for them a priori in the mind, and must therefore be capable of being considered apart from all sensations.*
>
> (A20/B34)

Space and time are not abstracted from sensory experience in the manner of empirical concepts, but must be presupposed as a condition for having any experience at all. Otherwise, given sensations would have no place or time to be. That there is such a spatio-temporal order, and indeed a necessary one, is clear to Kant: sensations are ordered in sequences, one after the other in time, and one next to the other in space, following the laws of mathematics and geometry.

Kant elaborates his view in a series of arguments, of which two exemplary ones are as follows:

> *Space is a necessary a priori representation, forming the very foundation of all outer intuitions. It is impossible to imagine that there should be no space, though we might very well imagine that there should be space without any objects to fill it. Space is therefore regarded as a condition of the possibility of appearances, not as a determination dependent upon them. It is an a priori representation which necessarily precedes all outer appearances.*
>
> (A24/B39)

> *Time is a necessary representation which underlies all intuitions. We cannot take away time from appearances in general, though we can well take away all appearances from time. Time therefore is given a priori. In time alone is all reality of appearances possible. These appearances may all vanish, but time itself (as the universal condition of their possibility) cannot be eliminated.*
>
> (A31/B46)

These two complementary arguments allow us to appreciate the Kantian philosophical method of separating layers of any given phenomenon to reveal its underlying structures. Here, he observes that given some object, we can imaginatively separate the space and the time in which the object is situated for independent consideration. Once we perform this abstraction, we can see that without the spatio-temporal form, there can be no object to perceive. The object depends upon the spatio-temporal form, but the spatio-temporal form does *not* depend upon the object. This is the crux of the argument. The spatio-temporal form is therefore independent and prior to the objects within it.

For Kant, we can think of time in general without specifying any particular events, and we can think of space in general without specifying any objects contained in it. Empty space and empty time are conceivable, and moreover, are such that we must conceive of them *as the very conditions* under which we can have any experience at all. With such reflections, Kant maintains that space and time are within us before we experience any objects.

Insofar as space must be presupposed as the condition for any outer experience, and insofar as time must be presupposed as the condition for any experience, Kant refers to them as knowable *a priori*. They are forms of the mind prior to sensory experience that each human has identically, and that order our sensations into a common and objective form. He refers to space and time in technical terms as *a priori* forms of sensibility.

Kant draws amazing conclusions from this examination of space and time, which bear long reflection:

...everything which is perceived in space and time, therefore all objects of an experience possible to us, are nothing but appearances, that is, mere representations which, such as they are represented, namely, as extended beings, or series of changes, have no independent existence outside our thoughts.
(A490-491/B518-519)

> ...space and time [are] determinations and relations which are inherent in the form of intuition only, and therefore in the subjective nature of our mind, apart from which they could never be ascribed to anything at all.
>
> (A23/B37-38)

> It is therefore only from the human standpoint that we can speak of space, extended objects, etc. If we depart from the subjective condition under which alone we can have outer intuition, that is, so far as we ourselves may be affected by objects, the representation of space means nothing whatsoever.
>
> (A26/B42)

> Time is therefore simply a subjective condition of our (human) intuition...and in itself, apart from the subject, is nothing.
>
> (A35/B51-52)

> We deny that time has any claim on absolute reality, so that, without taking into account the form of our sensuous condition, it should by itself be a condition or quality inherent in things ...
>
> (A35-36/B52)

> ...the things we perceive are not in themselves what we perceive them as being, nor are their relations in themselves such as they appear to us, so that, if we remove the subject or the subjective form of our senses, all qualities, all relations of objects in space and time, indeed space and time themselves, would disappear.
>
> (A42/B59)

3 How are (some) synthetic *a priori* judgements possible?

We described earlier how Kant's theory of judgement augments Hume's elementary distinction between 'relations of ideas' and 'matter of fact' with the additional distinction between knowing a judgement to be true *a priori*, versus knowing it to be true *a posteriori*. The result is to generate a new kind of judgement, previously unheard of, that informatively adds some new content to the subject – i.e., the judgement is synthetic –

but is knowable to be true independently of experiencing the objects to which that judgement refers. From the standpoint of philosophical theorizing these judgements are desirable, for they are informative and yet necessarily true.

We previously used as an example of a synthetic *a priori* judgement, 'all events are caused'. This contrasts with 'all effects are caused', which is true as a matter of definition, where the judgement's truth can be determined merely by analysing the relationships between the meanings of the terms. We also noted how Kant listed some other judgements as synthetic *a priori*, namely, those in geometry and mathematics. We are now able to provide Kant's answer to the grand question of how synthetic *a priori* judgements in geometry and mathematics are possible.

It is obvious to Kant that geometry is the science of spatial relationships, and that as its body of knowledge it has a set of necessarily true propositions. These include the statement that on a flat surface, the sum of the interior angles of a triangle equals 180°. Also included is the statement that on a flat surface, parallel lines never meet.

These statements do not seem to be mere matters of definition, as if one could change the relationships arbitrarily and decide that on a flat surface, parallel lines *will* eventually meet! Kant's challenge is to explain how such statements can be necessarily true, if they are not arbitrary matters of definition.

His answer, as we can now imagine, is that the synthetic *a priori* quality of space itself is being expressed and presented in the synthetic *a priori* quality of the statements that describe space's geometrical relationships. The synthetic *a priori* propositions of geometry are possible, because space itself is knowable *a priori* as a feature of the human mind – one that informs our sensations with an 'outer' empirical reality. Geometry expresses the very nature of space. Kant states accordingly that 'our explanation is thus the only explanation that makes intelligible the possibility of geometry, as a body of *a priori* synthetic knowledge' (A25/B41).

In a similar way, he explains the synthetic *a priori* quality of mathematical propositions such as *2988 + 8749 = 11,737*.

(His own example is the more elementary $7 + 5 = 12$.) Here, one cannot arrive at the sum 11,737 by examining the meanings of '2988', 'plus', and '8749', as we are able to do, for example, in deciding that the statement 'this bachelor is unmarried' is true. In the latter case, we only need to examine the meaning of the word 'bachelor'. In contrast, Kant says in relation to $7 + 5 = 12$, 'we may analyse our concept of such a possible sum as long as we will, still we shall never discover in it the concept of twelve' (B16). Mathematics, he concludes, is composed of informative synthetic judgements, rather than uninformative analytic ones.

Kant also maintains that mathematics is grounded originally upon the basic number sequence '1, 2, 3, 4,...'. Realizing that the passing of time implicitly contains such an enumeration (and we can add that as a continuous 'flow', the structure of time implicitly contains the continuum of numbers as well), Kant maintains that time expresses itself in the structure of the number line. Arguing in parallel, since time is knowable as an *a priori* feature of the human mind that gives order to our sensations, mathematics is also knowable *a priori*. Since both space and time prescribe orderings to our sensations before we have any sensations, they have a synthetic quality, telling us *a priori* how our experience must be structured.

Key idea: Why mathematics and geometry work in the daily world:

Since space and time organize sensory information that is given to us, and since geometry and mathematics articulate the very structures of space and time, our experience must always have a geometrical and mathematical form.

4 Some objections to Kant's theory of space and time

Kant's theory of space and time is innovative, if not revolutionary. It is also controversial. Perhaps the most fundamental objection issues from the abstractive, scientific style of thought he uses to identify the nature of space. Kant asks us, in effect, to consider any ordinary object, imagine that it is not there, and to continue this process of dissolution until all of the objects in the physical world are imaginatively set aside, leaving us to think exclusively about the pure, empty space in which the objects had been situated, as devoid of all content, and as a form on its own. Kant believes that it makes sense to think of space in this fully detached and evacuated way, while admitting that we can never experience space as such. It remains unclear, though, whether we can actually construct a conception of such a space.

Another objection stems from the overall state of knowledge when Kant was living. For Kant and his generation, 'logic' meant Aristotelian logic and 'geometry' meant Euclidean geometry. This led him to assert accordingly that 'space has only three dimensions' (B41), never imagining that there could be higher dimensions of space, or spaces that are described by alternative geometries. One can consequently ask whether human experience needs to be organized according to the rules of Euclidean geometry as Kant could only believe.

One reply to this objection is to define a more generally Kantian position acknowledging space as a form of the human mind, but adding that this form is completely general, inclusive of all higher dimensional and non-Euclidean spaces. Some people claim to experience a kind of enhanced consciousness in the apprehension of higher dimensional spaces, but if one follows this Kantian line of thought, the implication would be that when people claim to experience higher, non-Euclidean dimensions of space and perhaps even a kind of enlightenment thereby, that they would be equally as far from the absolute truth as before, since space in general, of whatever dimension, yields knowledge that remains human, all-too-human.

Spotlight: Non-Euclidean geometry

During the 1800s, non-Euclidean geometries challenged the universal validity of the Euclidean system that had prevailed for the previous 2000 years. The pioneers were Nikolai Lobachevsky (1792–1856) and Bernhard Riemann (1826–1866) who developed geometries based on hyperbolic and spherical surfaces respectively. The geometry of a spherical surface is easy to visualize, since we can picture the spatial relationships as if we were piloting an airplane across the earth's surface, or travelling along the surface of a bubble.

Suppose we were to fly in a large triangle starting from the North Pole straight down to a point on the equator, and then straight along the equator for some distance, then making a right angle to turn northwards to return directly to the North Pole. In doing so, we will have traced a great triangle, where the two of angles touching the equator together measure 180º. Adding the third angle at the North Pole yields a triangle whose interior angles amount to more than 180º. This contradicts the Euclidean maxim that the sum of the interior angles of a triangle must equal 180º.

This reason for the discrepancy is that although the non-Euclidean space in the example is a thin, two-dimensional surface, like that of a bubble, and like that of a Euclidean plane, it is not flat, but curved. Questions consequently arise concerning the validity of Kant's claim that space – and he was indeed thinking of only of 'flat' space – is necessarily true as the only possible geometry. Subsequent theoretical physics has shown that the geometry of non-Euclidean, curved space more accurately represents the space of our physical universe.

Dig Deeper

Henry Allison, *Kant's Transcendental Idealism: An Interpretation and Defense*, Part Two, Section 5 (Yale University Press, 1983)

Lorne Falkenstein, *Kant's Intuitionism: A Commentary on the Transcendental Aesthetic* (University of Toronto Press, 1995)

Paul Guyer, *Kant and the Claims of Knowledge*, Chapter 16 (Cambridge University Press, 1987)

Arthur Melnick, *Space, Time and Thought in Kant* (Kluwer Academic Publishers, 1989)

Lawrence Sklar, *Space, Time and Spacetime* (University of California Press, 1977)

Study questions

1. Briefly characterize Newton's conception of space and time, and explain why Kant found it objectionable.

2. Why is Kant's characterization of space in an intermediary position between Newton's and Leibniz's characterizations?

3. Why does Kant believe that space and time are not concepts?

4. Why does Kant believe that space and time are not derived from sensory experience?

5. How does Kant argue that space and time are knowable *a priori*?

6. What does Kant mean when he says that all things intuited in space and time are only appearances? Of what are they appearances?

7. Why does Kant claim that if we depart from the human standpoint, then space and time represent nothing at all?

8. How does Kant use the structures of space and time to explain how synthetic *a priori* judgements in geometry and mathematics are possible?

9. Do you think that it is possible to think of space or time without any contents at all?

10. Why does Non-Euclidean geometry pose a challenge to Kant's theory of space? How might Kant answer the charge that his theory of space is mistaken, because it is based on a Euclidean conception of space?

5

Aristotelian logic: the structure of the faculty of understanding

Kant's views on space and time were philosophically revolutionary, but his insight reaches an even deeper level by using Aristotelian logic to explain how we further construct our world of daily experience. In this chapter we will see how Kant begins with twelve elementary logical forms of judgement, and how he extracts from them twelve pure concepts which serve to organize our given sensations. These are the 'categories' or pure concepts of the understanding. One of these categories is the concept of 'causality', which will help Kant explain in reply to David Hume's scepticism, why we can indeed rely upon our scientific theories to predict the future.

1 Aristotelian logic

One of the leading ideas in the history of Western philosophy is that human beings are rational animals. They are, of course, also laughing animals and political animals, featherless, walking on two legs. Such features notwithstanding, along with self-consciousness, rationality has been the famously human essential characteristic in Western philosophical theorizing.

Kant inherits this tradition, but by the time he is writing in the late 1700s, philosophers regarded the idea of rationality as best expressed by the discipline of formal logic – a discipline that Aristotle first formulated which, like algebra, uses letters and symbols to refer to and to designate abstract connections between concepts, individuals, relations and the propositions that contain them as elements. We are already familiar with this style of thinking from the elementary formula *S is P*, which represents a judgement such as 'the sky is blue', or in this case more directly, the thought of a 'blue sky'. We are all born as rational animals, and as such, the elementary forms of logical judgement – that is, Aristotelian logic itself – are present within us as a matter of human nature.

When Kant develops his theory of knowledge, he makes extensive use of the idea that our human nature is logical. Utilizing a kind of 'faculty-based' psychological model, to recall, he distinguishes two sectors of the mind that participate jointly in the formation of knowledge. The first is the faculty that receives sensations and organizes those sensations according to spatial and temporal forms, the faculty of 'sensibility', which we discussed in the previous chapter. The second is the faculty of 'understanding', which applies concepts to those sets of organized sensations, so we can apprehend the sets of sensations as things of a particular kind, which we will now consider.

The faculty of sensibility supplies the intuitions, or individuals, and the faculty of understanding supplies the concepts, which give meaning to the individuals which the faculty of sensibility has initially configured in space and time. Neither faculty stands alone: 'concepts without content are empty, intuitions without concepts are blind' (A51/B75), as Kant says. When these two faculties operate together harmoniously, elements from each faculty are effectively situated to combine with each other into judgements of the form, 'this individual is of some particular quality', following the elementary logical format, *S is P*. Through such an act of judgement, our consciousness registers the apprehension of, say, a 'blue sky'.

Before any sensations are given, both faculties are assumed to have their own structures fully intact, knowable *a priori*, comparable to the structure of a car's motor, before it is started. The structure of sensibility is constituted by the forms of space and time, which we can imagine as two endless and intersecting expanses of infinitesimal points, like empty containers, waiting for some sensory content to fill them. Kant refers to these formal infinite expanses as 'manifolds' of spatial and temporal intuition. They are merely sets of contentless points to be filled with sensations, soon to be given meaning through the application of concepts. In the last chapter, we saw how Kant specifies the structure of the faculty of sensibility in the section of the *Critique of Pure Reason* entitled the 'transcendental aesthetic'. He specifies the structure of the understanding, or faculty of concepts, in his discussion of 'transcendental logic'.

In principle, Kant finds the structure of the understanding easy to describe. Recognizing that we are essentially rational animals, and that our rationality is expressed most generally and precisely in the discipline of formal logic, he adheres closely to the steadfast structure of Aristotelian logic, highly respected and unchanged substantially for two thousand years. Kant consequently utilizes the twelve elementary forms of judgement, stated in the logic books of his time, and bases his theorizing on this specific set of judgements. In the *Critique of Pure Reason*, he presents the following 'table of judgements', constituted by twelve basic logical structures which he believes all human beings, insofar as they are 'rational animals', use to think rationally:

Logical forms	Examples
A Judgements of quantity	
1 Universal	*All roses are red*
2 Particular	*Some roses are red*
3 Singular	*This rose is red*
B Judgements of quality	
1 Affirmative	*This rose is red*
2 Negative	*This rose is not red*
3 Infinite	*This rose is non-red*
C Judgements of relation	
1 Categorical	*This rose is red*
2 Hypothetical	*If this is a rose, then it is red*
3 Disjunctive	*Either this is red, or this is not red*
D Judgements of modality	
1 Problematic	*This rose may be red*
2 Assertoric	*This rose is red*
3 Apodeictic	*This rose must be red*

Kant attends mainly to the different logical aspects of our thinking as listed in the left-hand column above. Taking a look at the table, we can note that the same judgement, *This rose is red*, has four logical aspects, like different coloured lights that one can shine upon the judgement. The judgement is at once singular, affirmative, categorical and assertoric. These logical aspects – twelve of them in all, organized into four groups of three – occupy the centre of Kant's attention when he theorizes. He uses them as a template throughout his philosophy as a way to lend a systematic form to his discussions.

Key idea: Table of judgements:

This is a listing of twelve elementary logical forms of judgement, taken from the logic books of his day, through which Kant identifies the basic formats in which we think rationally.

Kant's project in this particular section of the *Critique of Pure Reason* is to employ the above table of logical judgements as a guide to describing the fixed, universal structure of the faculty of human understanding. As we know, the understanding is a faculty of concepts that applies concepts to objects, individuals or 'intuitions' given to consciousness through the faculty of sensibility. The fixed structure of the understanding therefore contains a set of *basic concepts* that are always applied to given intuitions, informing them with a rudimentary organization, somewhat in the way a hot waffle iron informs the soupy batter into a hard, gridlike shape before one adds any syrup, butter, whipped cream or fruit.

Kant isolates the faculty of understanding and describes it in the abstract, independently of any sensory contents that might be given by the faculty of sensibility. Since he is characterizing the understanding as it is by itself, independently of sensory experience, the fundamental concepts that he identifies as constituting the understanding are empty, devoid of sensory content. Kant refers to them as formal or 'pure' concepts, just as the forms of space and time are originally empty. All in all, they are sets of formats for sensations.

Kant's discussion of the fundamental concepts of the understanding proceeds initially with an account of how these concepts apply to the empty forms of space and time – the containers that receive the sensory impressions to begin with. With that established, the way is marked for the application of the pure concepts to specifically sensory-filled configurations in space and time, such as a lamp, window, wall or doorway.

To see how Kant informatively uses the table of judgements, it is important to understand how he defines the idea of a 'concept'. For him, a concept is an expression of unity among a set of representations. The many points of light in a clear night sky, for example, can be comprehended together under the concept of a 'star'. The concept 'star' allows us to apprehend all of the points of light as being of the same kind. In contrast, although they might also see the individual points of light, a dog or cat looking up at the same sky will not comprehend all of the points of light in this way, since neither animal has the concept of 'star'.

Kant refers technically to a concept as the 'common representation' under which a unity of various representations is brought. By 'representation', he means either an intuition or a concept, so the common representation 'star' would bring together under itself the set of individual points of light, or intuitions, of the various individual stars.

The key thought is that a concept is an expression of unity amongst a set of representations. A set of pure concepts inherent to the faculty of understanding would thus be a set of unifying functions that organize whatever is given to the understanding by the faculty of sensibility. At the most basic level, the concepts of the understanding prescribe the most basic kinds of unity to space and time in the abstract, considered as sets of empty points, or 'manifolds'. In such an abstracted situation, we would be talking about how the concepts of the understanding organize the structure of space and time with respect to any given object at all, or with respect to an 'object in general'. Kant is interested here, not in the conditions for apprehending this or that kind of an object, but the conditions for apprehending *any* object. He is interested in the 'conditions for the possibility of human experience', as he describes it.

Another word that Kant uses to express the idea of a unifying function is 'synthesis', since this conveys the idea of taking up a set of individuals and connecting them together into a unity. He also uses the word 'combination' to express the same idea. Kant's German word for this is *Verbindung*, which signifies 'binding together', as in a community, society, union or association. He consequently describes the pure concepts of the understanding as various modes of synthesis or combination. In sum, the pure concepts of the understanding are various modes of synthesis of the manifolds of intuition provided by the forms of space and time.

This is a technical way to express Kant's idea, but the underlying thought is as follows. Considering the human mind – not in connection with any specific sensory experience, but only in relation to the formal structures it has prior to any sensory experience – to be like a computer fresh from the factory, or a car immediately rolling off the assembly line, we have two faculties, the faculty of sensibility and the faculty of intuition, each with its respective formal structure. The structure of sensibility gives us two empty containers, space and time, constituted merely by sets of points that constitute an endless expanse. These forms are empty, like cups without any liquid in them, or sheets of paper with no writing. They are nonetheless constituted by a 'manifold', which is a set of points that waits to be filled with sensory content and further organized.

Conjoining with space and time, we have the understanding – a complementary faculty of pure concepts that works with sensibility to organize the more specifically configured manifold of space and time, once it receives some sensory information. As a faculty of 'concepts', the understanding projects twelve different ways in which objects in general, given in space and time, are organized both with respect to their individual constitution and with respect to their interrelationships with other objects.

Note how we are still not yet referring to any specific sensory objects such as the silver lamp, or ballpoint pen, or leafy tree, but are still speaking in the abstract, of any objects whatsoever that could be given as possible configurations in space and time, prior to their being actually given. We are thinking about the structures that must operate within any possible human experience, quite universally. The investigation is about how the mind operates at the most fundamental level, as if we were talking about how the various parts of a car's motor are related to each other, prior to turning on the motor.

To some people, this style inquiry could sound premature, or backwards, or impractical, or unrealistic. It might even sound too cautious and fearful, as if to avoid drowning, Kant is trying to learn first, how to swim 'in theory' before touching the water. These kinds of criticisms have sometimes been levelled at Kant's method.

If, however, we consider the work of engineers, it stands that if the exact engineering specifications of a car's parts are indeed known, one can calculate how fast it will drive before it is even built. This is the kind of inquiry, by analogy, in which Kant is engaging. Like an engineer who is building a spacecraft, and who can calculate before the spacecraft is launched, how it will be able to perform, Kant, thinking like a scientist, is trying to specify how the mind works in general before it knows anything specific. He is aiming to specify for any given human, including the humans that have not yet been born, exactly how powerful the human mind is.

In the *Critique of Pure Reason*, Kant is keen to establish once and for all, how powerful human reason actually is, because some philosophers have maintained optimistically that we can know fully about the ultimate realities of the universe, such as whether God exists, while others have maintained sceptically that we cannot even be sure whether or not the sun will rise tomorrow or that the water will boil again when we heat it.

2 The pure concepts of the understanding

How, then, does Kant use the table of logical judgements to characterize the fundamental activity of the understanding and to answer this difficult question about the human mind's power? How does he use this table to extract a corresponding list of pure concepts that the understanding uses to organize the spatio-temporal manifold for the sake of experiencing any object at all? The answer is that Kant 'reads off' of each kind of logical judgement a pure concept that matches the meaning of the judgement. Some of the correspondences are easy to see. Some are less obvious.

Let us consider one of the clear cases to illustrate what Kant has in mind. On the table of judgements, among the judgements of 'relation', there is the logical form of the 'hypothetical judgement, sometimes called a 'conditional' judgement. The format is *if A, then B*, as in 'if the water's temperature is 100°C, then the water will boil' or as in 'if one smokes too many cigarettes, then one will damage one's lungs'. Through these examples it is easy to see that the elementary form of logical judgement, *if A, then B*, when applied to the world's factual details, expresses the concept of 'causality'. Since we are rational beings and think inherently in terms of the format *if A, then B*, we also thereby think in terms of the concept of causality, rather inevitably.

In his extraction of pure concepts such as 'causality' from the table of judgements, it should be more evident now, how Kant uses the discipline of formal logic to develop a theory of the structure and limits of human experience. These pure concepts, or 'categories', of the understanding, amount to the various ways in which the human mind organizes, or binds together, the spatio-temporal manifold. Kant asserts that there are no other ways, and that these are the necessary ways, since we are logical beings who have no choice but to think according to basic logical forms, just as a cat has no choice but to think like a cat, or a dog, like a dog.

Here is the list of pure concepts or 'categories' of the understanding that Kant sets out. It follows the table of judgements exactly.

General logic: Forms of logical judgement		Transcendental logic: Pure concepts of the understanding (the categories)
A Judgements of quantity		
1 Universal	→	1 **Unity**
2 Particular	→	2 **Plurality**
3 Singular	→	3 **Totality**
B Judgements of quality		
1 Affirmative	→	4 **Reality**
2 Negative	→	5 **Negation**
3 Infinite	→	6 **Limitation**
C Judgements of relation		
1 Categorical	→	7 **Substance**
2 Hypothetical	→	8 **Causality**
3 Disjunctive	→	9 **Reciprocity**
D Judgements of modality		
1 Problematic	→	10 **Possibility**
2 Assertoric	→	11 **Actuality**
3 Apodeictic	→	12 **Necessity**

Spotlight: Aristotle's categories

Aristotle, thinking philosophically and seeking accordingly the most general and most universal way to understand the world, formulated a set of concepts that apply to any given object. He was the first systematically to do so. These concepts, one can say, characterize an 'object in general': any object must be a substance of some shape and kind, in some place at some time, in a certain position, appearing a certain way, acting on some other things, and being itself acted upon by some other things. Standing as an inspiration to Kant, Aristotle offered a list of ten basic concepts, or 'categories':

1 Substance (e.g., a man; a horse; 'Edward')
2 Quantity (e.g., five feet high)
3 Quality (e.g., talkative)
4 Relation (e.g., taller than; shorter than)
5 Place (e.g., on the street corner)
6 Time (e.g., Tuesday afternoon)
7 Position (e.g., sitting; standing)
8 State (e.g., having clothes on; holding a book)
9 Action (e.g., talking to someone)
10 Affection (e.g., being spoken to)

Kant confirms that his purpose in formulating the set of categories is essentially the same as Aristotle's. He also criticizes Aristotle for not having formulated his list of categories in a systematic way, and for only having employed his philosophical insight to construct the list. By relying upon the established inventory of elementary forms of judgement from the logic books of his own time, Kant was confident that his list of categories was more solidly grounded than Aristotle's.

It is telling that later thinkers such as G. W. F. Hegel (1770–1831) levelled the same kind of criticism at Kant's own list of categories. Unimpressed with Kant's having lifted his set of categories from a logic book – and there were indeed controversies at the time of whether there were exactly twelve basic forms of judgement or a different number – Hegel required that any list of categories should be derived with a greater sense of necessity. He argued that each category should derive from the one preceding, as a plant grows from a seed in stages. Inspired by Kant's initial efforts, this is the ideal towards which Hegel aims in his own logical works.

The table of logical judgements in the *Critique of Pure Reason* is not a structure to be passed over. Kant uses this table as a guide for organizing some of his most important discussions, almost like an architectural plan that he applies throughout his philosophy. The clearest example is the first 22 sections of the third *Critique*, the *Critique of the Power of Judgement*, where Kant analyses the judgement, 'this object is beautiful'. Here, he considers the judgement at length from the four different logical angles prescribed directly by the table of judgements, namely, according to quality (Sections 1–5), quantity (Sections 6–9), relation (Sections 10–17) and modality (Sections 18–22).

We can say in general that the reliability of logical form serves as one of Kant's great intellectual supports. Not only does he use the table of judgements to structure his discussion of judgements of beauty, he structures the *Critique of Pure Reason* in the format of traditional logic books of the time. These books begin typically with a discussion of singular 'concepts', move on to an account of dual combinations of concepts, or 'judgements', and then conclude with an examination of tripartite combinations of judgements, or 'syllogisms'. With respect to the latter, as we will see, Kant describes the structure of metaphysical speculation in reference to the forms of syllogisms, which are three-part logical sequences where two judgements imply a third, as in (1) 'All people are mortal', (2) 'John is a person' which implies (3) 'John is mortal'. It was noted earlier that Kant's philosophy is inspired by astronomical thinking. He is also moved by a tremendous respect for the elementary structures of Aristotelian logic. Astronomy and Logic are two hands that fundamentally shape his philosophy.

Key idea: Categories of the understanding:

For each of the twelve logical forms of judgement, Kant discerns a pure concept, or category. Each pure concept expresses the application of the respective logical form of judgement to given sensory stimuli, defining a specific way to integrate and organize the stimuli into a world of objective experience.

Study questions

1 What is the difference between the faculty of sensibility and the faculty of understanding?

2 Kant states that 'concepts without content are empty, intuitions without concepts are blind'. With respect to the faculties of understanding and sensibility, what does he mean by this?

3 What is a 'concept' according to Kant?

4 What does Kant mean by a 'manifold'?

5 How does Kant describe the process of 'synthesis' or 'combination'?

6 Why is the table of judgements important for understanding other parts of Kant's philosophy?

7 How does Kant arrive at the set of twelve categories from the table of logical judgements?

8 What is the difference between Aristotle's understanding of 'categories' and Kant's understanding of them?

9 Why do some philosophers find Kant's style of thinking to be unrealistic? How might one reply to such criticisms?

10 Why are astronomy and logic inspirations for Kant's philosophy?

6

The transcendental deduction

The transcendental deduction or 'justification' of how pure, non-sensory, universalistic categories of the understanding can apply necessarily to what seems to be their very opposite – namely, individual, contingently-occurring sensory items – is one of the most difficult and innovative segments of the *Critique of Pure Reason*.

This chapter will discuss the two versions of the transcendental deduction – the 'A' version of 1781 and the 'B' version of 1787 – explaining how, through successive acts of organizing sensory stimuli, we construct the world around us, or what is usually called 'nature'. Central to the transcendental deduction is our sense of self, or 'I', which is at the basis of all our systematizing mental processing. The chapter will conclude with a reference to how in the 'B' version, Kant contrasts limited, receptive human awareness with God's unlimited, creative awareness.

Upon encountering the phrase 'transcendental deduction', it could be assumed that Kant is attending to a logical relationship, as when 'deducing' that if some shape is an equilateral triangle, then that shape must also be a figure, closed with three sides, each of which is a straight line of identical length. The term 'deduction' might also invoke an image of Sherlock Holmes, since he solved crimes by using logical deduction. Given the importance of logic for Kant, 'transcendental deduction' *seems* to refer to a logical deduction of a transcendental sort.

In the transcendental deduction of the categories, this is not how Kant uses the term 'deduction'. The history of legal reasoning supplies us with a different meaning, and Kant has this legal sense in mind when he discusses the transcendental deduction.

'Deductions' were published by governmental authorities in the German and surrounding kingdoms to justify legal positions on serious questions, often when the issue was volatile enough to lead to war. The practice began in the late 1500s and soon reached the point where the deductions became long and elaborately printed, with thousands published between the 1600s and 1800s. By entitling his discussion a 'deduction', Kant invokes the legal tradition to reinforce the intellectual gravity and sobriety of his inquiry.

The style of reasoning involved in legal deductions recalls the general search for presuppositions that we described in Chapter 1. We saw that Kant often argues 'backwards' by starting with an established fact to reveal the necessary presuppositions of that fact. Similarly, if a question were to arise over the rights associated with a tract of land, for instance, a legal deduction would work 'backwards' to trace the history of ownership to identify the original titleholder. In this respect, Kant's procedure in transcendental argumentation – a procedure which likewise traces a proposition back to its source – can be appreciated as being modelled upon the history of legal thinking. We have seen how Kant thinks like an astronomer and logician. He also thinks like a lawyer.

The term 'deduction' here means 'justification' or 'legitimation' in answer to the question, 'With what right?' do the categories of the understanding apply to experience, and moreover, apply necessarily to experience. The question emerges because as 'pure' concepts, the categories lack sensory content. When considering in contrast, concepts derived from experience – empirical concepts – these clearly have the right to apply to experience, for they are extracted from experience itself. Tracing empirical concepts back to their respective sense impressions reveals their 'birthright', or 'genealogy'. We cannot trace the pure concepts of the understanding back to any sense impressions, however, since they do not derive from any sensory experience. They exhibit a necessity and universality that sensory experience itself can never express.

Since the pure concepts of the understanding do not arise from sensory experience, Kant's question is why they should apply to sensory experience at all! Establishing this connection and application is the project of the transcendental deduction. He aims to describe how, as a requirement for producing knowledge, the faculty of understanding – the faculty which contains the categories – *gives rules* to the faculty of sensibility, without which there would be neither knowledge nor experience. Since the understanding is a faculty of concepts, the transcendental deduction aims to justify how the categories apply to experience, both in general and necessarily. For Kant, 'knowledge' is 'a whole in which representations stand compared and connected' (A 97). This definition reveals one of our main concepts in the transcendental deduction: it reveals that at the core of the deduction is the notion of 'connection', or what he also calls 'combination" (*Verbindung*) and more technically, 'synthesis'. Knowledge requires synthesis, which is the crucial concept.

The first edition of the *Critique of Pure Reason* was published in 1781; the second edition appeared six years later in 1787. Between the first and second editions, Kant reworked the transcendental deduction, giving us two complementary renditions of the same project to think about. These are commonly referred to as the 'A' (first edition) version and the 'B' (second edition) version. We will consider each in turn.

1 The transcendental deduction: first edition, 'A' version

Let us begin our exposition with some reflections on an ordinary experience. Suppose that we are watching a baton twirler performing. The twirler is spinning the baton, tossing it up into the air, catching it, passing it behind her back so that it briefly goes out of sight, moving it up and down, sideways, and in all sorts of directions, all very rapidly. Consider, as we watch, how the image of the baton on the back of one's retina parallels the baton's movements, never at rest, sometimes disappearing, and then suddenly returning, and so on. Nothing about the retinal image of the baton stands still, as the tiny linear shape spins round and round, appearing, disappearing and then appearing again. The full episode produces several series of discrete and different images on the retinal surface. This describes the raw perceptual situation, or set of sensory inputs from the twirling baton.

Note how throughout the rapid changes of the baton's image, one nonetheless says to oneself (perhaps one has seen the performance before), 'the girl is twirling the baton'. In having this thought, one is applying to the dynamic sensory situation, the concept of 'baton', which does an interesting job: it effectively holds together and stabilizes the experience of the baton's movement. If one were to attend mainly to the concept applied, thinking that one already understands these performances and knows all-too-well how they typically unfold, it could be easy to overlook the particular sensory nuances of the performer's baton twirling on this occasion. With such a conceptually focused mentality, and through it, having grasped the essence of the situation early on, the performance might soon become unexciting and monotonous.

Within this scenario, the concept of the baton functions importantly to introduce a dimension of constancy, predictability and familiarity into the perceptually dynamic presentation. This function becomes especially evident if one keeps in mind the fluctuating movements that, moment to moment, are being presented on the back of everyone's retina who is watching the twirling. The concept of 'baton' operates cognitively to 'freeze' the twirling object's movement by holding together all at once in a single intellectual summary, the object's series of changing positions. To 'hold together' in this way, is literally to comprehend the baton's movements.

Kant extends this idea and considers our daily experience as a whole. In doing so, he recognizes that our experience is always held together by a vast array of concepts, mostly empirical ones. In the present situation with the baton twirler, we have concepts operating such as 'baton', 'person', 'grass', 'stadium', 'people', 'sky', 'car', 'pole', 'light', 'shirt', 'seat', 'crowd', and 'cheering'. Without such concepts, and many others like them, our experience would be nothing but 'one great blooming, buzzing confusion', to use the words of the philosopher William James (1842–1910), who had in mind an infant's preconceptual impression of the world.

Since raw perception is a manifold of sensation in perpetual flux, Kant concludes that any stabilities or constancies of which we are aware in ordinary perception must arise from our own activity of holding together that sensory manifold into certain forms. *We ourselves* stabilize the flux of raw perception into recognizable objects which maintain their integrity through time. Such is his main idea. Our application of concepts to experience makes possible the ordinary perception of objects such as the baton.

In the first edition version of the transcendental deduction, Kant describes this process of how we hold together our experience in three steps. He begins by asserting that in any act of perception we must first hold together some given set of sensations to form a rudimentary image. In the above example, this would be an initial grouping of sensations into a linear form – the straight-lined figure of the baton – that is distinguishable from the background surroundings. This is the initial 'apprehension' of the item that we will soon recognize as a baton. To complete the awareness of this item, we need to remember or 'reproduce' the linear images from one moment to another, so that the previous presentation of the linear form coheres in continuity with the present impression of it. This yields an awareness of the 'same' baton as existing through a series of moments. Finally, we comprehend the baton as a kind of thing by applying the concept of 'baton' to the complex image. To perceive the baton as such we need consequently to (1) apprehend the basic linear image, (2) hold together as similar, a series of those linear images over time, and (3) apply a concept to this set of linear images to comprehend the series of images as referring to a kind of thing, and indeed a single object in which all of our images refer and cohere.

Each of the three stages involves a 'putting together' of elements or, as Kant describes it, a 'synthesis'. This activity of synthesis is the work of our own consciousness in its effort to make sense of the manifold of sensations, and in the longer view, to make sense of the world as a whole. In technical terms, Kant characterizes the first stage as a *synthesis of apprehension* whereby we form an initial image, the second stage as a *synthesis of reproduction* whereby we hold together a series of images to form a composite image of the thing over time, and the third stage as a *synthesis of recognition in a concept* where we apply a concept to the composite image and comprehend it as a kind of object.

Key idea: Synthesis:

Kant maintains that after receiving sensory stimuli, the mind extensively processes the stimuli, aiming to stabilize them for comprehension. For example, it organizes the stimuli into perceivable objects and assigns to them spatial and temporal locations. At the centre of this mental processing is the spontaneous and creative act of 'binding together' various elements. Kant refers to this process as synthesis, or combination.

In this threefold synthesis, the imagination does a great deal of work. Kant states accordingly, not to mention provocatively, that 'imagination is a necessary ingredient of perception itself' (A121n). With this realization, he maintains that the faculty of imagination underlies all awareness of the world and all knowledge. It is a faculty that stands in relation to both the faculty of understanding, which supplies concepts (as in the 'synthesis of recognition in a concept') and the faculty of sensibility, which supplies intuitions (as in the 'synthesis of apprehension' and the 'synthesis of reproduction'). The faculty of imagination integrates and harmonizes our understanding and our sensibility in the threefold synthesis that produces ordinary experience.

Appreciating at this point how the process of synthesis is fundamental to constructing our experience, Kant reaches a crucial point: he now seeks the ultimate origin within ourselves of these stabilizing projections or 'syntheses'. In this search for the ultimate ground of synthesis, he seeks an aspect of our mind which is (1) unchanging, since the various syntheses introduce stability and the source of these syntheses must therefore itself be stable and abiding, (2) active, since the syntheses are productive by introducing stability into what otherwise would be a constant and incomprehensible flux, (3) non-sensory and knowable *a priori*, since the syntheses need initially to produce pure concepts of the understanding as well as the intuitions of space and time, all of which are knowable *a priori*, (4) an expression of pure unity, since in the activity of synthesis of whatever kind, this is the feature that our mind is projecting.

It takes some penetrating philosophical insight on Kant's part to discern what aspect of the mind fits the above description. According to Kant, the ultimate source of synthesis is revealed by the very awareness we have of being the same person over time. The foundation of all knowledge is expressed in our self-awareness. Today, for instance, when I think about the last several hours, it is clear to me that it was 'me' who did this or that a few hours ago. Thinking of my longer term past, it was still 'me' who played in the schoolyard many years ago. It has been one and the same person all along, namely 'me', who has had these experiences over the years. It has been no one else. I do not experience your experience, and you do not experience my experience.

The formal structure underlying one's self-awareness is exactly the same in everyone. It can be expressed by saying that for any thought one has, it is always possible to say to oneself, 'that is "my" thought'. This deeper, formal dimension of the self is independent of any particular experience and is knowable *a priori*. Kant refers to it as a 'pure unchangeable consciousness' and in technical terms, as 'transcendental apperception'. In one respect, although it is not passive, it is nonetheless like an empty container into which all of one's experience is comprehended, just as space and time are like empty containers. As the source of all synthesis, and hence, of all stability in our experience, Kant maintains that this transcendental apperception, or basic awareness of oneself as being 'me' throughout, 'is the *a priori* ground of all concepts' (A 107).

As the ground of *all* concepts, it is the source of both pure concepts of the understanding and empirical concepts. Kant maintains that this fundamental sense of self is the most basic unity of all, regarding all other unities as the *projection* of this self. These projections include all concepts and intuitions, since each has an integrity of its own. All objects of awareness are thereby regarded as projections of one's own integrity as a fundamentally unified consciousness. In the history of philosophy, this thought is revolutionary.

Key idea: Transcendental unity of apperception:

This is the fundamental unity of the mind which, in everyone, underlies the awareness that one's experience is of 'me' or is 'mine'. It is the source of all synthesis, and hence, that which ultimately gives each of the objects of perception their individual, stable identity.

To appreciate further the meaning of Kant's notion of the transcendental unity of consciousness, we can consider the thought of an 'object in general'. If we think of what this phrase could mean, there is a reference to some integrated entity, but not much else besides. An 'object in general' is a kind of blank, although it is not nothing at all. We are thinking of a 'something', but of a 'something' completely unspecified. Keeping this in mind, let us consider ordinary experience to fill out this idea of an 'object in general'.

Several people are in a room, all looking at a large clock on the wall. Each person sees the clock from a different angle. A few leave the room and then later return. The 'clock' remains on the wall throughout each person's experience as the 'same' object. In this sense of 'object', there is the thought of a thing in space and time to which each person's perceptions refer when looking at or talking about the clock. This is all a matter of common sense, and when Kant talks about the meaning of the term 'object', he has this familiar idea in mind of a thing that remains stable throughout a series of various perceptions.

One of Kant's repeated lessons from his examination of British empiricism is that what is given to us in sensory experience carries no necessity with it. It is possible, he muses, that the objects around us could change their colour suddenly, that water might boil at different temperatures every other hour, that our foods could nourish us one day, but not the next. The world could be, or could become, an incomprehensible chaos, if all we had to rely upon philosophically were that which is given through sensation. The British empiricists, believing that the mind is initially blank, and that our experience both begins and arises from what is given in sensation, arrived at precisely this sceptical position, the very position against which Kant is reacting. The sheer fact that the water keeps boiling at the same temperature each day, that our food continues to nourish us, and that the air continues to sustain us, is enough to motivate opposition to the sceptical view.

Kant was sure that empiricism and its associated scepticism are mistaken, since he showed that geometry and mathematics are not derived from the contingencies of experience, but are disciplines constituted by propositions knowable *a priori*, universally applicable and necessarily true. With this inspiration, and having seen how to derive the universality and necessity of geometry and mathematics from the subjective forms of space and time, Kant sought further for subjective sources of other universal and necessary structures within our experience. These he found in the pure concepts of the understanding. A central feature of the transcendental deduction is to show that as well, the pure concepts of the understanding, or categories – and perhaps the clearest examples of categories are the concepts of substance and causality – are rules that determine very generally, the structures of objects within our experience. As 'rules' they organize and thereby unify, or bind together, the various sensory presentations that occur in space and time.

The crux of the transcendental deduction, then, is in Kant's observation that raw sensations do not present any unity by themselves, and that for us to know anything, we need to organize the raw sensations into discernable objects, as done through the synthesis of apprehension and the synthesis of reproduction. Despite these syntheses, which might still leave us with a set of objects without any predictable organization between them, Kant asks further, how is it possible that experience contains any necessary connections between the various objects we construct, and that we are not nonetheless facing an unpredictable chaos, as the empiricist view implies?

His answer refers us to the formal structure that underlies our fundamental sense of self, the transcendental unity of consciousness. His view is that at the core, this unity of consciousness is the source of all stability and synthesis. The pure concepts of the understanding then follow as the more determinate, logical expressions of this unity, which express specific kinds of necessary connection (e.g., as in causality). The application of these pure concepts of the understanding to the sensory objects that are presented to us in space and time, organizes those objects into an elaborate system that we call and appreciate securely as *nature*. The imagination, as the general principle of synthesis, connects the understanding and the sensibility. Kant summarizes the situation as follows:

We have therefore a pure imagination as one of the fundamental faculties of the human soul, on which all knowledge a priori depends. Through it we bring the manifold of intuition on one side in connection with the condition of the necessary unity of pure apperception on the other. These two extreme ends, sense and understanding, must be brought into contact with each other by means of the transcendental function of imagination, because, without it, the senses might give us appearances, but no objects of empirical knowledge, therefore no experience.
(A124)

The result of the transcendental deduction is the recognition that all relationships of necessity in experience ultimately derive from our own understanding, as it organizes the sensory presentations that are given to us through the categories and the forms of space and time. The 'laws of nature' are the reflections of our own understanding. As Kant says accordingly:

> *It is we therefore who introduce into the phenomena which we call nature, order and regularity. Nay, we should never find them in nature, if we ourselves, or the nature of our mind, had not originally placed them there.*
>
> (A125)

In the end, there is little within our experience for whose appearance we are not ourselves responsible. The sensory qualities that we experience (red, blue, green, etc.) are invoked by the interaction of what exists independently of us with our receptivity, the space and time in which those qualities are situated, are themselves forms of our own mind, the necessary interconnections between the sensory objects that we call 'nature', is a product of our understanding, and the very concept of an 'object in general', is a projection of the unity of our consciousness and sense of abiding self. There is a distinct sense in Kant's view, that when one apprehends a table, or chair, or a star, one can say, *'that is me'*.

Spotlight: One of Kant's few jokes

As consistently serious as Kant's writings happen to be – the discussion in the transcendental deduction is typical – he does entertain us with the following joke in setting out his theory of laughter in the third *Critique* (Section 54):

An Indian, at the table of an Englishman in Surat, seeing a bottle of ale being opened and all the beer spill out, changing then into foam, displayed his great amazement with many exclamations, and in reply to the Englishman's question 'What is so amazing here?' answered, 'I'm not surprised that it's coming out, but by how you were able to get it all in there [!]'

Kant characterizes laughter as 'an affect resulting from the sudden transformation of a tension-filled expectation into nothing'. We can read the above joke and perhaps consider some of our own, and think about whether Kant's 'relief theory' of laughter is on the right track. In contemporary literature, two other theories of humour compete with the relief theory, namely, the 'incongruency theory' and the 'superiority theory'. The first locates the causes of laughter in the perception of certain kinds of mismatches or irrationalities. The second is inspired by the experience of laughing 'at' something, rather than laughing 'with' it.

2 The transcendental deduction: second edition, 'B' version

Returning now to Kant's more serious side, the second edition version of the transcendental deduction modifies and sharpens the first edition version, as well as enhances it with some additional perspective. Kant begins with the assertion that 'all combination [i.e., synthesis] ... is an act of the understanding' and that 'we cannot represent to ourselves anything as combined in the object, without having previously combined it ourselves' (B130).

This retains the idea from the first edition version that all synthesis is a product of the subject's activity, but shifts the central activity of synthesis over to the understanding from the imagination, which now plays a subordinate role. By locating synthesis primarily in the understanding, the synthetic activity becomes more of an immediate manifestation within the understanding itself, of the fundamental ground of all synthesis, the transcendental unity of consciousness. Kant refers to the transcendental unity of consciousness as the 'original combination' (B133), thus rendering the understanding and its categories into a direct expression of our self-awareness.

The centre of attention in the second edition is the elementary relationship – one of necessity – between the unity of consciousness and the objects of which consciousness is aware. For us to have knowledge, the objects of which we are aware must be related to our unity of consciousness. Otherwise we could not be aware that we were aware of any objects. So rather than speak of the transcendental unity of *consciousness*, Kant emphasizes in the second edition that the unity under consideration is a transcendental unity of *self-consciousness*. From the notion of necessity involved in the relation between this self-consciousness and anything of which it is aware, Kant extracts the implications that he requires for the transcendental deduction, for he seeks an account of how the pure concepts of the understanding relate necessarily to sensory intuitions.

As in the first edition version, Kant focuses on the origin of 'objectivity'. This notion is marked by the difference between saying that some body, say, a large stone, is heavy, and saying merely as a personal report, that if I lift the body, it feels heavy to me. The notion of objectivity, along with that of an 'object', locates the heavy quality in the stone itself, and not in my subjective impressions of the stone. Objectivity involves thinking that 'stone' and 'heaviness' are 'combined in the object, no matter what the state of the subject may be' (B 142). Objectivity is thereby expressed in the judgement 'the body is heavy'.

In the second edition, Kant explores this idea more explicitly, looking for the source of all judgements that express objectivity. Such judgements express stability and ultimately, necessity, so the answer to the question of how objectively valid judgements are possible returns Kant quickly to the forms of logical judgement and the pure concepts of the understanding which express those forms.

This all establishes a much tighter connection between (a) the transcendental unity of self-consciousness as the original source of combination, (b) the understanding as the faculty of combination, (c) the table of logical judgements and the categories as expressions of various kinds of necessary connection, and (d) the manifold of given sensation that is organized according to the forms of space and time, which for any knowledge to be possible, must be in necessary connection with one's sense of self. The core of Kant's argument is given in Section 20:

> *The manifold which is given to us in a sensuous intuition is necessarily subject to the original synthetic unity of apperception, because by it alone the unity of intuition becomes possible (§ 7). That act of the understanding, further, by which the manifold of given representations (whether intuitions or concepts) is brought under one apperception in general, is the logical function of a judgement (§ 19). All the manifold, therefore, so far as it is given in an empirical intuition, is determined with regard to one of the logical functions of judgement, by which, indeed, it is brought into one consciousness in general. Now the categories are nothing but these functions of judgement, so far as the manifold of a given intuition is determined with respect to them (§ 13). Therefore the manifold in any given intuition is naturally subject to the categories.*
> (B143)

Kant adds that the above statement establishes a 'beginning' for the transcendental deduction of the pure concepts of the understanding. This could be puzzling, since he already seems to provide here a solid and sequential explanation of how the categories apply to sensory intuitions. What Kant believes that he has only done so far, though, is explain how the categories apply generally and validly to the forms of space and time, as they stand as manifolds of empty points, without any further determination or added sensory content.

His next step, then, is to explain how the categories apply to space and time when these forms are filled with actual sensory content. Within this richer context, the categories will be functioning to establish necessary relationships between sensory objects, such as causal relationships between them. This sets the parameters for the laws of nature, or as Kant says, for 'making nature possible' (Section 26). To complete the transcendental deduction along these lines, Kant now adds some further nuance to his argument.

Let us return to the baton twirling example to see this. Initially, the synthesis of apprehension presents us with an integrated linear form (the baton) within the structures of space and time. Without the forms of space and time originally in place, one could not synthesize the image of the baton to begin with, since there would be no place or time for the baton to be.

Reflecting now at a higher level of generality on the very nature of space and time, Kant notes that insofar as we are aware of space and time as single individuals that are filled with empty points, we must also have integrated, or synthesized, space and time *into* such individuals. This reveals a process of synthesis more fundamental than the integration of the small, localized bits of sensory information into the baton, as in the example. This more fundamental process of synthesis is none other than that described in the excerpt from Section 20 above, namely, that all manifolds are integrated ultimately by the transcendental unity of self-consciousness, which expresses itself in terms of the logical forms of judgement and subsequently, the categories of the understanding.

In the first edition version, the faculty of imagination plays a leading, close to central, role. In the second edition, its role remains essential, but it is more circumscribed. Kant here characterizes the imagination as being involved mainly in sensibility insofar as it synthesizes raw sensations into sensory individuals in space and time. As an active, productive function, it is not a merely receptive capacity, though, as is true for sensibility in general. As an active function, imagination is also associated with the understanding and with the fundamental processes of syntheses that derive from the transcendental unity of self-consciousness, as noted above. Kant speaks of the productive imagination as 'an effect of the understanding on the sensibility' (B152), thus retaining the idea that the imagination serves importantly as an intermediary between the understanding and sensibility.

With such thoughts in mind, Kant accounts for the necessary connection between the categories and any given sensory intuition, such as the baton in our example. Since the transcendental unity of self-consciousness's fundamental act of synthesis is expressed variously by syntheses expressed by the categories, and since this fundamental act of synthesis also operates to integrate space and time themselves into individuals on a grand scale, and to produce particular sensory

images (such as our baton), any specific sensory individual
that is presented in space and time must also be subject to
the syntheses expressed by the categories. In this respect, the
transcendental deduction is 'completed' in explaining how
the categories of the understanding must be brought into play
when apprehending an image of, say, a twirling baton. Kant
summarizes this situation in a footnote:

> In this way it is proved that the synthesis of apprehension, which
> is empirical, must necessarily be in accord with the synthesis
> of apperception, which is intellectual and is contained in the
> category completely a priori. It is one and the same spontaneity,
> which in the one case, under the name of imagination, and
> in the other case, under the name of understanding, brings
> combination into the manifold of intuition.
>
> (B161n).

Generally speaking, the second edition version of the
transcendental deduction differs from the first edition version
in its rhetorical tone. In the first edition, Kant is interested
positively in showing how we ourselves produce 'nature'
through the above-described synthetic activity of consciousness.
In the second edition, he describes the same, but notes that the
account only works if we suppose that the transcendental unity
of self-consciousness is an empty form, indeed the most empty
of forms. It is devoid of sensory content, it is unchanging, it
is an active unity, and it is necessary, but that is all. Without
some sensory inputs given by the faculty of sensibility, we have
nothing to think about and cannot know anything.

To convey how the transcendental unity of self-consciousness is
empty and dependent upon given sensations, Kant refers in the
second edition periodically and contrastingly to an alternative
style of consciousness, far more powerful, which by means of
its thought alone, specific objects of knowledge would come
into existence. This would be a divine consciousness, which
upon the very thinking of an object would render the object
into an existent reality, as in how God is thought to have made
the world through a mere act of thought. Such a divine being

would not fundamentally be an empty container that needs to receive some input from without itself, as is true for human beings. It would be a fully creative, self-sufficient being. Such a being would not need to receive sensory intuitions as we do, but would create its own intuitions through the activity of its own intellect. Humans, Kant emphasizes, lack this capacity for 'intellectual' intuition. We are restricted to sensory intuition, which must be given from without. The second edition of the transcendental deduction thereby articulates a more intense and explicit message of human finitude.

Dig Deeper

Henry Allison, *Kant's Transcendental Idealism: An Interpretation and Defense*, Part Two, Sections 6 and 7 (Yale University Press, 1983)

Eckart Förster (ed.), *Kant's Transcendental Deductions: The Three 'Critiques' and the 'Opus postumum'* (Stanford University Press, 1989)

Paul Guyer, *Kant and the Claims of Knowledge*, Part II (Cambridge University Press, 1987)

Béatrice Longuenesse, *Kant and the Capacity to Judge: Sensibility and Discursivity in the Transcendental Analytic of the Critique of Pure Reason* (Princeton University Press, 1998)

Robert Pippin, *Kant's Theory of Form*, Parts 4 and 6 (Yale University Press, 1982)

Study questions

1 In the transcendental deduction, does Kant use the term 'deduction' to signify 'logical deduction'? Why or why not?

2 What is the main purpose of the transcendental deduction of the categories?

3 Why is the term 'synthesis' important in understanding the nature of knowledge?

4 What is the difference in the role of the 'imagination' in the first edition and second edition of the transcendental deduction.

5 Describe, using an example, the threefold synthesis of the imagination. What is the relationship between the threefold synthesis and empirical knowledge?

6 What does Kant mean when he says that we ourselves create 'nature'?

7 What does Kant mean by an 'object in general'? What is the relationship between the 'transcendental unity of self-consciousness' and an 'object in general'?

8 Why does it make sense to say, in Kant's view, 'that is me', when one sees a table or chair?

9 What are some ways in which the second edition version of the transcendental deduction differs from the first edition?

10 How does sensory intuition differ from intellectual intuition?

7

Substance, causality and objectivity

Kant's 'synthetic principles of pure understanding' describe how each category of the understanding provides a necessary structure to our experience. Using the table of logical judgements as a guide, Kant considers the categories in four groups of three, structuring his discussion accordingly into (1) Quantity (Axioms of Intuition), (2) Quality (Anticipations of Perception), (3) Relation (Analogies of Experience), and (4) Modality (Postulates of Empirical Thought).

This chapter will review how each of the categories structures our experience, emphasizing the categories of relation in the Analogies of Experience. Widely discussed among Kant commentators have been the First and Second Analogies, which attend respectively to the categories of substance and causality. The chapter will conclude with a characterization of Kant's Refutation of Idealism, which has also received much attention in scholarly books and articles on Kant.

Since the project of the transcendental deduction is to show how the pure concepts of the understanding apply necessarily to our sensory experience, one might expect Kant to include references to some of the pure concepts by name during this discussion. He does not do this, however. Without highlighting specifically any pure concepts in the transcendental deduction, he instead attends to the general problem of how concepts devoid of sensory content can apply to sensory experience, and how those concepts can apply necessarily. His concern is with what, at first sight, appears to be an unbridgeable gap between pure concepts and sensory intuitions. He addresses this question before explaining how any of the pure concepts, or categories, apply specifically to experience.

Kant accordingly waits until he has completed the transcendental deduction, before turning his attention to each category in sequence. In doing so, his procedure follows the logic books of his time, which, as noted earlier, begin with a treatment of singular 'concepts', continue to discuss dual combinations of concepts, or 'judgements', and conclude with an analysis of triadic combinations of judgements, or 'syllogisms', the basic patterns of logical inference.

Adhering to this format, Kant first completes the transcendental deduction, which falls under the heading 'analytic of concepts', since the deduction concerns the pure concepts of the understanding. The next section – the one we are presently considering – is the 'analytic of principles'. It concerns the transcendental judgements that involve the application of the categories to experience. The third major section of the first *Critique* is the 'Transcendental Dialectic', which is structured upon syllogistic patterns of reasoning. We will discuss the Transcendental Dialectic in the next two chapters, in the context of Kant's account of the ideas of 'soul', 'world' and 'God'.

In terms of method, Kant sets the three logical divisions of 'concepts', 'judgements' and 'inferences' into a one-to-one correspondence, respectively, with the three faculties of human knowledge, 'understanding', 'judgement' and 'reason'. The parallelism reveals how, as a whole, the *Critique of Pure Reason* is constructed upon the logic books of his time. Moreover, as expressed in his three *Critiques*, Kant's philosophy as a whole is similarly inspired by this parallelism. The first *Critique*, the *Critique of Pure Reason*, investigates the power of the understanding. The second, the *Critique of Practical Reason*, concerns the power of reason in relation to morality. The third, the *Critique of the Power of Judgement*, reveals in relation to judgement, how the first two *Critiques* cohere, insofar as the third *Critique* confirms the compatibility between understanding and reason in reference to beauty and living things. The third *Critique* thereby enhances Kant's expression of the compatibility between natural science and morality, and correspondingly, between determinism and freedom. The following excerpt, with which Kant starts the 'analytic of principles', our present topic, reveals the connections between logical form and the faculties of human knowledge:

> *General logic is built on a ground plan that coincides exactly with the division of the higher faculties of knowledge. These are* Understanding, Judgement, *and* Reason. *Logic therefore treats in its analytical portion,* concepts, judgements, *and* syllogisms, *corresponding with the functions and the order of the above-named faculties of the mind, which are generally comprehended under the general name of the understanding.*
> (A131/B169)

As we know, the transcendental deduction establishes that the pure concepts of the understanding apply to sensory experience through the forms of sensibility, space and time, which serve as an intermediary. A three-step relationship holds, reminiscent of the tripartite form of a logical syllogism, where each statement's content partially overlaps with the next to determine a chain of reasoning. In the present case we have: (1) the categories are non-sensory, conceptual and *a priori* (i.e., universal and necessary), and they connect with (2) space and time, which are also *a priori*, but are furthermore sensory-receptive and individual, and these individual forms of sensibility in turn connect with (3) the sensory intuitions, which are individual, like space and time, but are *a posteriori,* (i.e., contingent, neither universal nor necessary). The pattern below shows how space and time are the connecting link between the pure concepts and the sensory intuitions:

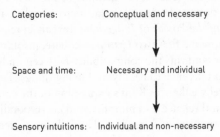

Categories: Conceptual and necessary

Space and time: Necessary and individual

Sensory intuitions: Individual and non-necessary

In view of the above relationships, Kant develops an account of how each category is associated with the form of time. Later, at various junctures, he will also introduce the form of space in connection with the categories, when considering the objective structures of the external world. Whereas space applies only to outer experience, time applies to all experience and is involved in the construction of every sensory item. Since Kant's project is the general one of showing how the categories apply to all possible experience, outer or inner, he initially unites the categories with the form of time, which applies to both outer and inner experience. Each category, when infused with a temporal dimension to render it compatible with experience, becomes a 'schematized' category. This temporalization modifies each category into a form determinate enough to prescribe the construction of sensory images.

The schematization, or temporalization – and one could even say 'aestheticization' (as in 'transcendental aesthetic') – of the categories is the preparatory condition for Kant's discussions of the 'synthetic principles of pure understanding', where he sets out within the context of sensory experience in general, and hence, within the context of the passing of time, the specific rules for experience that the categories supply. Again, inspired by logic and the table of judgements, his account divides into four parts, following the fourfold division of the table of the categories, which themselves derive from the table of judgements in general logic. His exposition is arranged in the following sequence:

1 *Axioms of Intuition*: concern the categories of quantity (Unity, Plurality, Totality)

2 *Anticipations of Perception*: concern the categories of quality (Reality, Negation, Limitation)

3 *Analogies of Experience*: concern the categories of relation (Substance, Causality, Reciprocity)

4 *Postulates of Empirical Thought*: concern the categories of modality (Possibility, Existence, Necessity)

In reference to the categories of *quantity* – unity, plurality, totality – Kant makes a straightforward claim in the Axioms of Intuition. He maintains the categories of quantity, as they inform the manifold of sensation, introduce the concept of 'number' into the sensations. Recalling and relying upon the notion of the synthesis of a manifold, he asserts that the categories of quantity entail that every sensory intuition must be a unity composed of a set of successively added, and previously given, parts. Constructed as such, each sensory intuition has an 'extensive magnitude'. The upshot is that 'all appearances are therefore intuited as aggregates' (A163/B204).

With respect to the categories of *quality* – reality, negation, limitation – the main claim in the Anticipations of Perception is equally straightforward. The notion of 'magnitude' remains, but complementing the 'extensive' magnitude that the categories of quantity contribute, the categories of quality introduce an 'intensive' magnitude into the field of sensation. By 'intensive magnitude', Kant means a 'degree' or 'intensity'. The categories of quality tell us *a priori* that all sensations must have a certain intensity, or degree, which can be located on a continuum. Every sensation can intensify, and can fade out. It makes no difference whether the sensation is of green or red, bitter or sweet, or, if we could perceive X-rays or other kinds of electromagnetic phenomena, what those experiences would be like. Of whatever kind they may be, every sensation must have a given intensity that could increase or fade.

When Kant considers the third set of categories, the categories of *relation* – substance, causality and reciprocity – his treatment offers far more detail and depth. These categories importantly introduce necessary and stabilizing relationships, or 'objectivity', into given sensory intuitions, and to establish this idea effectively, Kant devotes separate attention to each category in what he refers to as the 'Analogies of Experience'. The First Analogy is about the permanence of substance. The Second concerns relationships of causality, understood as necessary connections. The Third asserts the necessary interconnectedness between all things.

These applications of the categories prescribe necessary *relationships* between sensory intuitions, or, as in the case of the category of substance, the preconditions of those relationships. This is a departure from explaining in terms of magnitude, how sensory intuitions are constituted, as in the Axioms of Intuition and the Anticipations of Perception. Kant expresses this difference by saying that the Analogies of Experience describe how the categories of relation 'regulate' the patterns of sensory intuitions, as opposed to 'constituting' them. Their relationship to sensory intuitions is regulative, rather than constitutive.

In the First Analogy, Kant characterizes the structure of human experience that issues from the application of the category of substance to the sensory manifold. As the term 'substance' suggests, the structure is that of something which 'stands under' something else as a constant and reliable support. Specifically, this category introduces into the sensory manifold, a supportive permanent background for sensory qualities. For any series of sensory changes, if they are to be comprehended, then those changes can only be made sense of as the alterations of some underlying object, as when we say that the pot of water becomes hot when placed over a campfire. The category of substance organizes the sensory manifold into a field of objects in which our sensory qualities inhere, and in so doing, it establishes the thought of an unchanging substrate in which all sensory qualities inhere. In conjunction with the application of the remaining two categories of relation (causality and reciprocity), we call this substrate 'nature'.

Keeping in mind how as a form of sensibility, time is a precondition for all sensory experience and more specifically, how time infuses the categories in their schematic preparation to be applied to experience, Kant maintains that the category of substance when applied to the sensory manifold, expresses the constant presence of time. This refers to the single and abiding presence of time in every experience, rather than the fluctuation of sensory qualities that occur in time. He holds that if we did not project the notion of an object in which sensory qualities inhere – and the category of substance is responsible for this – then there would be no experience at all, since the field of sensations would remain disorganized. Hence his statement that 'permanence is thus a necessary condition under which alone appearances are determinable as things or objects in a possible experience' (A189/B232).

Kant's First Analogy helps to account for the peculiar experience of how, in our experience, it is always 'now'. For any human being, that human being's experience always takes place 'in the present' relative to that person. This is true for people's experience in the past, it is true for us, and it will be true for people in the future. When someone gazed at the starry skies ages ago, it was 'now' for them when it happened. Kant states that 'all existence and all change in time have thus to be regarded as simply a mode of the existence of that which remains and persists' (A183/B227). He is referring here manifestly to the objects in which sensory qualities inhere, but with the deeper note that 'change does not affect time itself, but only appearances in time' (A183/B226), it is a short step to associate time's permanence with that of an abiding object, as in the thought of a *nunc stans*, the 'standing still' of the present time.

In the First Analogy, Kant does not mention that the category of substance, like all of the categories, expresses the transcendental unity of self-consciousness, the ground of all synthesis. Recalling this connection, however, makes it more obvious that the permanent objects of experience in which sensory qualities inhere are, via the category of substance, none other than objectified projections of oneself as the subject of experience. In this respect, implicit in the First Analogy is the proposition that objects or 'substance' is identical with the subject of experience, as the objectification or projection of the subject. Subject and substance are identical in this sense.

A further upshot of the First Analogy is a useful distinction between 'change' and 'alteration'. A change occurs when one thing or quality goes out of existence and is replaced by another. An alternation occurs when a thing persists, but undergoes a change of quality. For example, with respect to a leaf's transition in colour from green to brown, one would say that the leaf's qualities change from green to brown, whereas the leaf itself undergoes an alteration of colour. In the broadest comprehension of sensory experience, Kant maintains that the projection of the category of substance onto experience as a whole entails that ultimately, there are only changes of sensory quality, and no changes in substance. To express this with greater profundity, he mentions the Latin phrase, *gigni de nihilo nihil, in nihilum nil posse reverti*, which translates as 'nothing comes from nothing, and nothing returns to nothing'.

Key idea: First analogy:

This is Kant's main discussion of how the category of 'substance' provides a structure to our experience. The structure is that of a stable, underlying object in which changing qualities inhere.

Spotlight: 'Nothing comes from nothing'

Kant's Latin phrase, *gigni de nihilo nihil, in nihilum nil posse reverti*, is from the Roman poet and satirist Aulus Persius Flaccus (34–62), in his third Satire. A century before, the philosopher Titus Lucretius Carus (99–55 BCE) wrote similarly in *The Nature of Things* that *Nil posse creari De nihilo, neque quod genitum est ad nihil revocari*, which translates as 'Nothing can be produced from nothing, and whatever has been made cannot be brought back to nothing'. The thought traces back to the ancient Greek philosophers writing before Socrates. Aristotle tells us in his book, *De caelo* that 'there are philosophers such as Melissus, and Parmenides, who deny any kind of generation and corruption. They say that nothing is really born or corrupted – it only appears to us to be so' (*De caelo*, iii, 1 298b15–18). The idea is that the world is eternal, stretching forever into the past and forever into the future, and that insofar as we have always been a part of this eternal being, and will always remain so, death is only a surface phenomenon. The principle seems obvious, but it does contradict the theistic idea that God created the world 'out of nothing'.

The Second Analogy concerns the application of the category of causality to all alterations in our experience of the external world. In the background is Hume's sceptical account of causality, against which Kant is reacting, which holds that since we can perceive no necessary connections between events, all events are loose and separate from one another, like a hand full of marbles. The Humean implication is that as far as we can know, anything can happen at any time. The boiling water on the stove could change into a dry Halloween mask, and the mask itself could change the next moment into an alarm clock, and so on. Since there is no causality as necessary connection, all experience could in principle be a complete and incomprehensible chaos. Kant aims in the Second Analogy to show, contrary to Hume, why this sort of chaos is not even a possibility for human experience.

Kant's argument is that certain features of our experience can be explained only if we assume the prior application of the category of causality. He agrees with Hume that the sensory manifold in its initial aggregation into perceivable items does not contain any necessity in its sequencing. We must, however, look further into ourselves to account for necessary conditions that experience might contain, for causality is not an empirical concept derived from experience.

To show that the concept of causality must be presupposed in our experience, imagine two different situations. First, consider that one is walking back and forth along a dock, following the length of a large ship. One walks along the ship's side from its front to its back, and then returns the same way to its front.

As one walks, the ship moves along within one's field of vision, with each of its sections passing by in sequence. The sequence of what one sees is reversible, since the sequence is only a function of how one initially chooses to walk.

Suppose further, though, that while one is walking along the dock, the ship sounds its horn and begins to pull out of the dock. The ship is again moving within one's visual field, but this time, the sequence of movements is not reversible. How it moves within the visual field is no longer subject to one's will. The ship is now moving independently, quite unlike how it moves when one's changes direction walking along the dock, or when one shakes one's head back and forth.

Kant asks how this difference in the sequencings is even possible. One sequence is subjective and one sequence is objective. His answer is that the difference between the two can appear in our experience, only if it is supposed that we are projecting a rule that allows us to assert, not of our subjective sequencing of experiences, but of the experiences insofar as they coalesce objectively in an object, that for any alteration, there is a preceding alteration from which a succeeding alteration necessarily follows. We must, that is, assume the projection of the category of causality, if we are to experience any objectively comprehended events or happenings. This causal rule applies to all events, and it precipitates a set of deterministic relationships between everything that happens objectively in space and time.

In saying that we must project the category of causality to experience any objectively comprehended events or happenings, Kant is asserting that the recognition of objects in causal relationships is a fundamental quality of our experience. It is so fundamental, that we need to presuppose its presence before we can account for any *subjective* sequence of experiences. We need to suppose that the ship is objectively at the dock to begin with, before we can decide to survey it by walking up and down the dock, or before we move it around in our visual field by shaking our heads back and forth when looking at it.

Consider how someone else at the other end of the dock, also surveying the ship, would have a different sequencing of his or her subjective experience of it. These differences would obtain for everyone who happened to be walking around on and within the ship, which stands substantially as the common object for everyone involved. In this respect, Kant states that we must 'derive the *subjective succession* of apprehension from the *objective succession* of appearances' (A193/B238).

Key idea: Second Analogy:

This is Kant's main discussion of how the category of 'causality' provides a structure to our experience. The structure is that of a necessary connection between events, which renders all scientific inquiry intellectually legitimate.

Kant turns next to the Third Analogy and the application to experience of the category of reciprocity, developing an observation from the Second Analogy. As we have seen, the Second Analogy focuses on the category of causality in connection with how certain sequences of our perceptions are not reversible. In this context, Kant reflects upon those sequences that *are* reversible, as when we walk up and down the dock viewing a ship, as opposed to watching the ship pull out of the dock. The Third Analogy develops the significance of our having reversible series of perceptions, and associates this feature of our experience with the application of the category of reciprocity.

The Third Analogy's main observation is that if we are able to reverse our series of perceptions – 'I can direct my perception first to the moon and then to the earth, or in reverse, first to the earth and then to the moon' (A211/B257) – then the perceptual objects involved must exist at the same time and be connected with one another. They must 'coexist', as Kant phrases it. For the possibility of such a reversible sequence of perceptions, there needs to be some spatial continuity and connection between the objects of perception, so that we can shift our attention between them as we will. Kant characterizes this continuity and connection as a 'community' between all objects in space that coexist, for 'without community each perception of an appearance in space is broken off from every other' (A214/B260) – a situation that would render the continuity of experience impossible.

Taken as a whole, the three analogies of experience explain how the temporalized categories of substance, causality and reciprocity, when applied to the manifold of sensations work to 'make nature possible' (A216/B263). They organize the sensory manifold into a unity, structuring it according to rules of necessary connection. The result is an experience determined by a hard structure of interconnected perceptual objects.

To complete the analytic of principles, Kant explains in the 'postulates of empirical thought' how the last three categories of *modality* – possibility, actuality, necessity – apply to the sensory manifold. In one aspect, his exposition is uncomplicated, constituted as it is by the direct translations of these three categories into the language of his theory of knowledge. Specifically, he characterizes what is 'possible' as whatever agrees generally with the conditions for having any intuitions at all. This provides a narrow sense of possibility, the import of which is that if an object cannot be given in experience or connected with it, then it is not possible. Here, 'possible' means 'within the sphere of possible experience'. Kant maintains similarly that what is 'actual' are those possibilities that are objectively bound up with sensation, and that consequently appear in experience. What is 'necessary' are those actualities that are considered as determined by the universal conditions for experience, in particular, causality.

In the course of these discussions Kant makes a claim about these modal concepts – possibility, actuality (or existence) and necessity – that reappears some chapters ahead when he addresses one of the traditional arguments for God's existence, the ontological argument. In our present section, he states that 'the categories of modality are distinctive insofar as in determining an object, they do not in the least augment the concept to which they are attached as predicates' (A219/B266). In reference to the category of actuality, for instance, Kant maintains that 'in the *mere concept* of a thing, there is to be found no mark of the thing's existence' (A225/B272). This precludes any arguments that start with a definition, or concept of some thing and go on to conclude from the concept alone that the thing exists. In Chapter 9, we will revisit this style of argument as it applies to the ontological argument for God's existence, which Kant accordingly criticizes.

In characterizing 'actuality', Kant states that what is given in perception is actual, along with anything that can be inferred from that perception according to the laws of causality. The possibility of drawing any such inferences supposes to begin with, that we have before us a world of things in space and time, objectively determined by laws of causality.

Aiming to reaffirm the presence of this world, Kant adds in the second edition a section entitled the 'Refutation of Idealism' that draws from the First Analogy's treatment of the category of substance, along with some additional concluding remarks. His purpose is briefly to refute Descartes' sceptical view that the existence of the external world is either 'doubtful and indemonstrable' or 'false and impossible' (B274). He is also responding to the inherent problem in the British empiricist view that the immediate objects of awareness are our ideas. If the latter were true, we could never be sure of what our ideas objectively represent, if we cannot step beyond the confines of our consciousness.

The First Analogy claims that for experience to be possible, our perceptual experience needs to have some stability. This is provided by the projection of the category of substance, which organizes the perceptual field into a set of objects in which sensory qualities inhere. Descartes argued that since he could not trust his senses, he was certain only of his own subjective existence, and that the existence of the external world was uncertain. In reply, Kant observes that Descartes' (and everyone else's) self-awareness has the quality of enduring through time, and he asks how this kind of enduring intuition of oneself as persisting through time, is possible. Kant's view is that one's own sense of permanence can only be a reflection of the permanence that we apprehend in the external objects we perceive. The transcendental unity of consciousness – a unity which we do not experience in its purity – expresses itself as the category of substance, which when applied to the sensory manifold generates a field of stable objects with qualities (e.g., tables and chairs). The perception of those objects provides the permanence that organizes our own self-perception in time, since all experience in time is determined by the category of substance. Thus, 'the consciousness of my own existence is simultaneously an immediate consciousness of the existence of other things outside me' (B276). We need to perceive the stable external objects at the outset, for us to have any self-knowledge, since the empty categories and the empty transcendental unity of consciousness within us cannot supply that knowledge by themselves. As Kant states, 'the categories are not *knowledge*, but mere *forms of thought*, by which given intuitions are turned into knowledge' (B288).

Kant's concluding remarks to the postulates of empirical thought, also added in the second edition, reinforce this refutation of idealism by introducing into consideration, the form of space as well. He adds that for any of the categories to express objective reality, we need intuitions that are 'in all cases outer intuitions' (B291). In reference to the category of substance in particular, he states that we require an intuition in space, 'for space alone can determine anything as permanent, while time, and therefore everything that exists in the internal sense, is in a constant flux' (B291). Once again, Kant's point is that if one has an intuition of oneself as permanent, then the permanence involved needs to derive from the apprehension of objects in space, and hence, from the external world.

Key idea: Refutation of idealism:

This is the principal location for Kant's argument that in order to have an explicit awareness of oneself as such, one needs to presuppose the existence of objects in an external world.

At this point in the *Critique of Pure Reason*, Kant believes that he has described in sufficient detail how our faculties of knowledge work together at various levels to establish the possibility and basic structure of human experience. To conclude the 'Transcendental Analytic', which was constituted by the 'Analytic of Concepts' and the 'Analytic of Principles' which we have just surveyed, Kant summarizes his results and adds some reflections to foreshadow the discussions that will occupy him for the rest of the *Critique*. These concern the implications of his analysis of our faculty of knowledge with respect to the perennial question of securing metaphysical knowledge, or knowledge of things in themselves.

He speaks here repeatedly of 'two worlds': the 'sensory world' of appearances, or 'phenomena', whose objects we can know, and the 'intelligible world' of ultimate reality, things in themselves, or 'noumena', whose objects we can never know. Underlying his discussion of phenomena and noumena is the central tenet of his theory of knowledge, that 'for us, *understanding* and *sensibility* can determine objects *only in conjunction*' (A258/B314). This reiterates what he said earlier in the *Critique*, that 'thoughts without content are empty, intuitions without concepts are blind' (A51/B75).

The mistake of previous philosophers, Kant states in 'The Amphiboly of Concepts of Reflection', is to regard sensations and concepts as reducible to one another, as if they had essentially of the same kind of being. To him, it is a philosophical dead end to maintain in principle, either that one can clarify all sensations into a set of precise concepts, as rationalistic philosophy aims to do, or to explain all concepts as derivatives from sensation, as empiricism attempts. The key to understanding Kant's outlook and criticism of philosophers such as Leibniz and Locke, is his firm recognition of a *distinction in kind* between sensations and concepts, or between individual entities and universal entities. We need to be given intuitions to render our concepts meaningful, and if the only intuitions we have are sensory, then our knowledge is clearly limited.

Dig Deeper

Henry Allison, *Kant's Transcendental Idealism: An Interpretation and Defense*, Part Three and Part Four, Section 14 (Yale University Press, 1983)

Gerd Buchdahl, *Kant and the Dynamics of Reason: Essays on the Structure of Kant's Philosophy*, Chapter 9 (Blackwell, 1992)

Paul Guyer, *Kant and the Claims of Knowledge*, Sections 8–14 (Cambridge University Press, 1987)

Arthur Melnick, *Kant's Analogies of Experience* (University of Chicago Press, 1973)

Eva Shaper and Wilhelm Vossenkuhl (eds.), *Reading Kant: New Perspectives on Transcendental Arguments and Critical Philosophy* (Blackwell, 1989)

Robert Stern, *Transcendental Arguments and Scepticism: Answering the Question of Justification* (Oxford University Press, 2000)

Study questions

1 Why is the parallelism between 'concepts, judgements, and inferences' and 'understanding, judgement, and reason' useful for understanding Kant's philosophy?

2 Why is it necessary to 'schematize' or 'temporalize' the categories of the understanding?

3 What are the four sections into which Kant organizes his discussion of the 'synthetic principles of pure understanding', and which categories are considered in each section?

4 Why are the categories which are discussed in the 'analogies of experience' especially relevant to establishing the objectivity of our experience?

5 How does the syllogistic structure of the transcendental deduction inform Kant's discussion of the schematism of the categories of the understanding?

6 In what sense do the categories referred to in the axioms of intuition and the anticipations of perception 'constitute' our sensory intuitions?

7 What is the difference between the subjective order and the objective order of our perceptions? How does the subjective order relate to the category of reciprocity? How does the objective order relate to the category of causality?

8 What is the difference between 'change' and 'alteration'?

9 What does Kant think of arguments that begin with simply a conceptual definition of some item, and argue from the definition itself that the item actually exists?

10 In order to become aware of ourselves, why must we presuppose that we perceive objects in the external world?

8

Metaphysical knowledge of the human soul

We are naturally curious about our ultimate metaphysical being. Some philosophers – a prime example is René Descartes – argue that we are thinking substances, that our inner being is simple, that it contains our personality, and that we can know ourselves independently of all physical objects.

In his discussion of the Paralogisms of Pure Reason, which this chapter will discuss, Kant maintains that each of the above claims is either unprovable or false. At the core of his arguments is the observation that all of our experience, both of the external world and of ourselves, occurs in time. As such, we can know only how we appear, and never as we absolutely are.

As we turn to the Transcendental Dialectic of the *Critique of Pure Reason* – a book that examines whether our capacity to think rationally is powerful enough to provide metaphysical knowledge – we should pause upon the section title, 'Pure Reason as the Seat of Transcendental Illusion' (A298/B355). It says that reason generates a kind of *illusion*. To appreciate the meaning of this suggestive section title, it is important to grasp how Kant distinguishes 'understanding' from 'reason'.

Through the application of pure concepts, the faculty of understanding contributes the basic intellectual form of all our experience. As the formal expression of the rational quest for knowledge, this faculty applies twelve logically based categories to given sensory manifolds to constitute and stabilize those manifolds into comprehensible experiences. During the course of the understanding's operations, various types of experiential sequences are put together. There are causal sequences amongst actual objects, sequences of thoughts in one's mind, and an overall awareness of everything as sequentially organized in one way or another. In principle, the sequences blend endlessly into one another. The most obvious cases are causal sequences, which extend into the past and future from whatever point we designate.

For Kant, the human mind is driven to comprehend the world and itself as maximally as possible. We always want to know more, and are disposed to extend what we know as far as we can, even if for the sake of greater comprehension, we go beyond what the evidence will support. The feature of the mind from which this effort to comprehend everything extends, is reason. It draws inferences, sometimes extensive, from the knowledge we already have. It seeks the ultimate truth and is relentlessly expansive.

As Kant describes it, reason aims for the highest unity of thought seeking 'to find for the conditioned knowledge of the understanding, the unconditioned, whereby the unity of the understanding is brought to completion' (A307/B364). Our reason essentially strives to uncover the absolute unity beneath the changing appearances in our experience. In this regard, Kant refers to the 'unity of reason'.

In the Transcendental Aesthetic and Transcendental Analytic, Kant argued at length that since our knowledge is conditioned by what is given in sensation, the nature of our intellect and the nature of our receptivity, it is impossible to know anything beyond space and time. Nonetheless persisting within this restricted cognitive environment is our reason, which generates the illusion that we can have knowledge of non-spatio-temporal realities. He states:

> *Reason is exclusively concerned with absolute totality in the use of the concepts of the understanding, and aims to carry the synthetic unity, which is thought in the category, up to the completely unconditioned.*
> (A326/B383)

Kant is aware that as humans, we ask perennially and inevitably about the nature of the self, the nature of the external world, and the nature of being in general, or God. In reason's speculations about the nature of self, world and God, logical inferences extend the categories of substance, causality and reciprocity to their ultimate and ideal point. These inferences, syllogistic in form, are all invalid in Kant's view, and they create the illusion that we can know the nature of the self, the world and God, when this is impossible.

Key idea: Our reason generates illusion:

For Kant, humans construct their experience according to spatial, temporal and logical forms that are inherent within us. We cannot knowingly go beyond these forms, but in a rational effort to know everything, we are disposed nonetheless to extend our logic beyond its legitimate bounds. These extensions generate illusions which make it appear that we can know what in fact, is impossible to know.

The three main segments of the Transcendental Dialectic – the total length of which is about 400 pages in the original edition, occupying the bulk of the *Critique's* second half – respectively address whether we can have metaphysical knowledge of the self, the world and God. 'The Paralogisms of Pure Reason' investigate the knowledge of the self as a permanent substance. 'The Antinomy of Pure Reason' surveys four questions related to the physical world's ultimate nature. 'The Ideal of Pure Reason' explores our knowledge of God's existence. These lengthy queries constitute much of the 'critique' of pure reason *per se*, since Kant is determined to show, based on the theory of knowledge he established in the *Critique's* first half, how incapable our reason is for providing ultimate answers to these philosophical questions that have haunted, and will forever haunt, human beings.

Spotlight: Dialectic

'Dialectic' is a style of inquiry which assumes that through the use of logic, we can advance towards truth by developing the conflict between opposing opinions. When two individuals debate logically over some question, intelligently struggling to establish which argument is closer to the truth, their dialogue exemplifies dialectic. As reasonable as it seems, sometimes the truth is more complex than a straightforwardly oppositional contest of opinion will admit, and it requires us to reconcile and assimilate aspects from each side of a debate into a more comprehensive understanding of the situation. The original 'either/or' style of dialectic can thus give way to a 'both/and' style. The latter introduces a new meaning of dialectic as the 'reconciliation of opposites within a more comprehensive perspective'.

As history has shown, the latter dialectics of opposition and reconciliation tend to become regimented into a mechanical and inherently expansive, three-step format, where one begins with some topic, or 'thesis', recognizes its opposite as an 'antithesis', and rather than trying to decide between the two in an exclusive way, amalgamates the opposing positions into a reconciliatory 'synthesis'. This synthetic result can then be taken as the initial 'thesis' of a further three-step sequence, the structure of which can be expansively reiterated over and over again until a grand synthesis eventually comprehends everything.

This notion of dialectic as the reconciliation of opposites is important in the German Idealist philosophies of Fichte, Schelling and Hegel, as well as in Marxism. Kant, however retains the original, more traditional, meaning of dialectic. In reference to questions that lead us beyond the realm of possible experience, he maintains in the Transcendental Dialectic that oppositional debate ends in a stalemate that never advances towards the truth.

1 The paralogisms of pure reason – the nature of the self

Kant defines a 'paralogism' as a 'syllogism whose form is fallacious, whatever its content might be' (A341/B399). A 'paralogism of pure reason' is a pattern of syllogistic reasoning that appears when the category of substance is used to unveil the ultimate nature of the self. Rather than achieving this revelation, the category's extension beyond possible experience generates unprovable assertions about our ultimate inner being. These are sometimes encountered in religious thought where it is maintained that our inner being, or soul, is a substance that is simple, personal and capable of existing independently of space and time. Descartes believed this as well. Kant admits that such assertions might be true, but he argues that we cannot prove them to be true.

Long ago, Aristotle defined a substance as that which has qualities attributed to it, but which is not in turn, attributable to something else. Substances are where the attributions end, and substances are 'primary' in this respect. The earth and the moon are primary substances, as different individuals in which qualities such as sphericity and solidity inhere. In the same respect, my judgements are features of 'me', but I am not a judgement. My judgements change, but I substantially remain the same, so it always appears to me. The judgements inhere in me as their primary support.

Such parallels suggest that in my ultimate being I am a thinking substance. Kant argues in the First Paralogism, however, that this inference is fallacious. Our faculties of understanding and sensibility are originally empty of sensory content: the transcendental unity of apperception (the 'I think' which is in principle attached to all of one's mental images) has no content, the pure concepts of the understanding have no content, and space and time have no content. To know anything at all – and this includes the experience of knowing oneself – the originally empty forms of understanding and sensibility require some sensory inputs to compose into an experience. Once this content is in place, though, everything known through the faculties of understanding and sensibility will only reveal the appearances of things in time and space, not the things in themselves.

Such appearances include the experiential knowledge we have of our inner being, so from our experience of self-awareness, nothing follows about the ultimate nature of that inner being. Whether or not it is a substance, or immortal soul, remains unprovable. Kant repeats this kind of argument throughout the Paralogisms, appealing to how our knowledge is always in time, and is thus only about appearances.

In addition to considering oneself as a thinking substance, it might also be thought that one's ultimate inner being is simple and unitary. This is the topic of the Second Paralogism. The rationale is simple: it is difficult to imagine a set of thoughts that could inhere in a consciousness that is *not* a simple being. Kant points out, however, that it is not impossible for there to be a set of thinkers which together form a single thought, as might happen in a group consciousness. The arrangement would be analogous to how an integrated set of finger movements constitutes the single movement of a hand that, for example, makes a fist, plays the piano, or flashes a two-fingered 'V' sign for victory.

Kant's opinion is that the motivation for people to assert the soul's simplicity is mainly to distinguish the soul from matter, which appears to be thoroughly composite, since they believe that such a distinction can establish the possibility of life after death. Again recalling his theory of knowledge, Kant finds the motivation misplaced. Since the material world is in space and time, it is only the *appearance* of some ultimate being that is in itself neither spatial, temporal nor material. Little is therefore to be gained in distinguishing the soul from matter, since matter is not an ultimate reality to begin with. As a potential threat to the existence of the soul, Kant regards matter as nothing to worry about.

The Third Paralogism challenges the common and natural thought that one's ultimate inner being is infused with one's personality. In daily life, it is undeniable that there remains a constant awareness of oneself as 'me' as the same person today that I was yesterday and the day before that, so it is easy to assume that the ultimate reality of oneself includes this 'me' as its permanent character or personality. These ideas present themselves when reflecting upon the post-death condition of other people and ourselves, as when imagining that a deceased family member's spirit is watching over contemporary happenings, or when people suppose that some newborn infant is the reincarnation of someone recently deceased. Kant does not find the proposition contradictory. He argues that the day-to-day sense of one's personal continuity does not prove that one's personality carries over into one's ultimate inner being.

The reason, now familiar, is this: the awareness of oneself as 'me' is an awareness in time, so as such, it is only an appearance of whatever one ultimately is as a subject. Kant suggests that it is (remotely) possible that ultimately, there instead could be a flow of different subjects that transfer their consciousness to each other, similar to how a ball, upon hitting another, transfers its energy to it. His point is that the ultimate subject of experience remains unknowable, since we always experience ourselves in time.

The Fourth Paralogism returns us to the themes of the Refutation of Idealism and the associated Problem of the External World. Here, Kant reiterates his rejection of the proposition, shared by many empiricists and rationalists alike during Kant's era, that each of us is immediately aware only of our mental images, and that the existence of the external world is consequently doubtful. In the present discussion, we learn more explicitly that Kant rejects this theory of perception in favour of a 'direct' theory of perception. In the latter, we apprehend external objects without the need for any intermediary, self-enclosing set of mental images (A371).

Kant's rationale is that since space itself is a form of our awareness, we directly apprehend objects in the space that our minds project. The objects that we apprehend are admittedly only appearances of things in themselves, but they are nonetheless perceived directly as having an 'outer' reality. The theory of perception based on the assumption that we are immediately aware only of our mental images is thus mistaken, based as it is on an ambiguity in the expression 'outside us'. As he states, the expression is 'unavoidably ambiguous, sometimes signifying what *as thing in itself* exists apart from us in itself, and sometimes signifying what belongs merely to outer *appearance*' (A373). Its 'directness' notwithstanding, it is important to keep in mind that Kant's direct theory of perception establishes an awareness of outer appearances, *not* of things in themselves. All in all, though, Kant is confident that there is no problem about the existence of the external world because the world's externality is of our very own making, stemming from our own projection of space.

As he showed in the *Refutation of Idealism*, Kant's deeper point in the Fourth Paralogism is to underscore how our self-awareness depends inextricably upon the supposition of an external world, and that it is impossible to know ourselves independently of that external world. With this claim, Kant implicitly criticizes Descartes's famous effort in the *cogito* ('I think, therefore I am') to know himself with certainty, under the assumption that there might be no external world.

When considering the Four Paralogisms as a whole, we are not left simply in a condition where the knowledge of our ultimate inner nature is denied to us. There is a bright side. Kant regards reason's inability to attain knowledge of things in themselves as 'a hint from reason, to turn our self-knowledge towards fruitful practical use, and away from fruitless and extravagant speculation' (B421). The revelation of the Paralogisms as invalid arguments clears the way for us to focus more productively on another side of our reason, namely, its role in moral awareness as a solid guide to practical life. As our examination of Kant's moral theory will show, he maintains that reason gives us an *a priori* foundation for action in reference to what we ought to do. In contrast to the sceptical spirit of the Paralogisms, Kant will postulate the immortality of the soul as a moral necessity, despite the absence of scientific knowledge of the soul's immortality.

Key idea: The failure of metaphysics shifts our attention to morality:

Insofar as Kant repeatedly maintains that metaphysical knowledge is impossible – as in the Paralogisms – he appears to be a sceptic. His positive philosophical project, however, is to emphasize our moral awareness in light of the inadequacy of constructing airtight logical proofs. This effort to highlight morality occurs throughout the second half of the *Critique of Pure Reason*.

Dig Deeper

Henry Allison, *Kant's Transcendental Idealism: An Interpretation and Defense,* Part Four, Sections 12 and 13 (Yale University Press, 1983)

Karl Ameriks, *Kant's Theory of Mind: An Analysis of the Paralogisms of Pure Reason* (Clarendon Press, 1982)

Andrew Brook, *Kant and the Mind* (Cambridge University Press, 1994)

Michelle Grier, *Kant's Doctrine of Transcendental Illusion*, Chapter 5 (Cambridge University Press, 2001)

C. Thomas Powell, *Kant's Theory of Self-Consciousness* (Clarendon Press, 1990)

Study questions

1   What is the difference between understanding and reason?

2   What is 'dialectic'? What are the two main kinds of dialectic? Why does Kant entitle this section of the book the 'Transcendental Dialectic'?

3   What are the respective topics of the Paralogisms of Pure Reason, the Antinomy of Pure Reason and the Ideal of Pure Reason?

4   The Paralogisms of Pure Reason discuss the self in relation to which category of the understanding?

5   There are four Paralogisms. Which aspect of the self does each discuss?

6   Why is it crucial for Kant's arguments in the Paralogisms to recognize that all of one's self-knowledge occurs in time? What is time in Kant's view? What kind of knowledge does it provide?

7   Does Kant believe that we can prove the theory of reincarnation to be true?

8   What, according to Kant, is the main reason why people assert that the soul is a simple being?

9   In what sense does Kant maintain a 'direct' theory of perception?

10   What consolation does Kant offer at the end of the Paralogisms?

9

Metaphysical knowledge of the world and of God's existence

Among Kant's more thought-provoking and controversial claims in the *Critique of Pure Reason* is that when seeking answers to fundamental questions about the world, our reason embroils itself in contradictions. He describes how reason turns upon itself the Antinomies of Reason, which we will discuss in this chapter.

Kant is also well-known in the philosophy of religion for his claim that the traditional arguments for God's existence – the ontological argument, the cosmological argument and the teleological argument – are all invalid. Central to Kant's position is his refutation of the ontological argument, which we will examine, with its often-cited claim that 'existence' (or 'being', as Kant phrases it) is 'not a real predicate.'

1 The Antinomy of Pure Reason – the nature of the world

One of Kant's more fascinating claims is related to the 'Antinomy of Pure Reason'. It is that when we apply our reason to solve certain fundamental questions about the world, reason inevitably comes into conflict with itself. One might expect otherwise that for any dispute, one can always expect stronger versus weaker arguments for one side or the other, where the stronger arguments render one of the sides definitively more plausible. For certain key philosophical questions, however, Kant does not find this to be the case. He instead likens the situation – one that has been continuing for centuries within the philosophical world in a warlike and fruitless manner – to a game wherein merely whoever makes the first move wins. The problem with these philosophical questions is that whoever goes first is arbitrary, with a perpetual and pointless series of battles as a result.

In the Antinomy of Pure Reason, Kant identifies four basic questions and four corresponding Antinomies over which philosophers have continually fought, showing that in the face of reason's equal support of both sides, the questions have no definitive answers. They are:

1 Does the world have a beginning?

2 Is the world composed of simple elements?

3 Are we free?

4 Does God (i.e., an 'absolutely necessary being') exist?

Starting with the First Antinomy, let us suppose that the world has no beginning in time. If so, then at the present moment, an infinite amount of time will have passed, with the present moment serving to complete the series. However, an infinite series can never come to an end, so it makes no sense to assert that an infinite series has passed. The world must consequently have had a beginning in time. If so, then before the world began, there must have been an empty time with nothing in it and nothing happening. But nothing can happen in an empty time, so the world cannot 'happen' at any particular moment within it. The world must consequently have had no beginning in time. In sum, if the world had no beginning in time, then the world had a beginning in time, and if the world had a beginning in time, then the world had no beginning in time. Reason thereby confounds itself with this question.

The Second Antinomy asks whether the composite substances in the world are composed of simple, indivisible substances, or atoms, or whether all substances are continually decomposable into smaller and smaller units, endlessly. To begin, suppose that no composite substances are made up of indivisible substances, and that they are endlessly divisible. If so, then the composite substances will have no ultimate constituents. Since, as composites, the composite substances are not themselves ultimate, to deny that simple substances constitute them renders it impossible for there to be any composite substances at all, for there is nothing self-subsistent or foundational that could then constitute them. The composite substances must therefore be made of simple substances. If so, however, then the simple substances must occupy space and be perceivable, at least in principle. Everything that is perceivable is an organized manifold, though, so if the simple substances are perceivable, then they cannot be simple, but manifold, which brings us around into a circle. If composite substances are not composed of simple substances, then composite substances are composed of simple substances, and if composite substances are composed of simple substances, then composite substances are not composed of simple substances.

The Third Antinomy follows the same pattern. Suppose that we are not free. If so, then the only kind of causality is the mechanical, physical causality between events according to the laws of nature, which includes all of our bodily movements. For any effect, there is consequently a series of causes which explains that effect, extending into the past endlessly. If the series extends into the past endlessly, however, then the series lacks a beginning or completeness and is thus insufficient to explain the effect. To explain the effect adequately, we must introduce another kind of causality – one that can begin a series of events spontaneously of its own accord – which is called freedom. If, however, we assume the presence of freedom, then this will interrupt the array of mechanical causal patterns according to natural laws, which is impossible, if the patterns of the natural world are to remain intact and the world is to remain coherent. Thus to make sense of the laws of nature, we must suppose that we are free, and if we suppose that we are free, we cannot make sense of the laws of nature, which, once again, is a contradiction.

The Fourth Antinomy considers the existence of 'an absolutely necessary being' or God, broadly defined. The subject here is not 'God' in the traditional sense, as a transcendent being beyond space and time, but that of a necessary being within space and time. The line of reasoning refers us once more to the natural, causal sequence of events. Since each event in the causal sequence is a contingent being, there must be a being that is not contingent, but necessary, to explain the presence of the set of contingencies. The set of contingencies occurs in time, so as its foundation, the necessary being must also be in time. A necessary being in time would be an 'uncaused' cause, however, whose presence contradicts the law of causality's requirement that every member of the series is caused by another prior member.

To avoid this difficulty, the necessary being might alternatively be regarded as the entire causal series, but this makes no sense, since the entire series cannot itself be necessary if no single member of it is necessary. Alternatively, the necessary being might be located outside of the series, but this makes it impossible for the being to act 'in' time to begin the series. In sum, if we suppose a contingent causal series of events, then there must be a necessary being that underlies the series, and if we suppose that a necessary being underlies the series, then contradictions arise that render such a necessary being impossible.

As with the Paralogisms, the Antinomies offer some consolation. Introducing the conclusions established in his theory of knowledge, Kant reiterates that 'the world' which we have been considering throughout these investigations is only phenomenal. It is the mere *appearance* of things in themselves and is nothing without us. In this respect, it is nonsensical for the First Antinomy to ask about whether *in reality*, the world had either a beginning *or* no beginning. Time is a form of the human mind, so there is no question of whether or not 'in itself' the world had a beginning. Similarly, the Second Antinomy's question about whether the substances we experience are 'in themselves' either one or many is misplaced. The substances are in themselves neither one nor many, for we have no knowledge of their nature as transcendental objects.

The Third Antinomy questions whether or not we are free. Kant replies that there is no need to choose here between mutually exclusive alternatives, since both options can be true in different respects. As phenomena, we are not free, but as things in themselves we may be free. Kant grounds his moral theory upon this double-aspected perspective, which we will examine later in more detail. Finally, the Fourth Antinomy asks whether in view of the causal chain of events in nature, there is a necessary being that supports the series of happenings. Kant's response is that although within the field of appearances there can be no necessary being, since the field of appearances is simply that, appearances, outside of the realm of appearances there is the possibility of a necessary being as an 'intelligible cause' of what we experience in nature.

Spotlight: 'Two worlds' versus 'one world'?

In his discussion of the antinomies and elsewhere, Kant often refers to the 'world of appearances' as opposed to the 'world of things in themselves', almost as if there were two different worlds. To understand his motivation for speaking like this, we can consider how in our ordinary thinking, light waves, which are *colourless* in themselves, travel through the air to stimulate our retinas and to produce, for us and in us, the experience of colour, as when we look at a bright white, shining star in the night sky. The star's whiteness *per se* is not 'out there' far away in space in the star itself, just as the sour taste of a lemon is not 'in' the lemon itself, as it hangs from the lemon tree branch, untasted.

Kant extends the above kind of example in a radical way. We directly apprehend the thing-in-itself (just as in the above example, we directly perceive the star or the lemon), and this mind-independent being appears to us as a set of spatio-temporal objects. The objects' very spatio-temporal quality compares to the whiteness and sourness in the above example, for according to Kant, space and time are not qualities of the thing-in-itself.

It is not, though, exactly as if these spatio-temporal appearances of the thing-in-itself constitute a completely separate 'world' of their own, just as the star's whiteness or the lemon's sourness in our original example do not constitute a separate world of their own. All of these appearances are *intimately* bound up with the mind-independent realities that stimulate them, just as our personal behaviour in the spatio-temporal world is intimately bound up with what we intelligibly and inscrutably are in our moral character.

One might consequently think that it would be better to talk about only one 'world' instead of two, but neither the 'two worlds' nor the 'one world' way of describing the situation is altogether satisfactory. The 'two' worlds phrasing fails to capture how the world of spatio-temporal appearances is closely bound up with the thing-in-itself; the 'one' world phrasing fails to capture how the mind-dependent qualities that we communally share, do indeed constitute an interconnected group of their own, which Kant calls 'nature', all of which, without our own presence on the scene, would otherwise disappear.

2 The ideal of pure reason – the knowledge of God

Reason, as we have seen, is a faculty that integrates our knowledge and seeks the ultimate truth. As an artifact of its effort to comprehend everything, the idea of God emerges. God is describable variously as that which 'possesses all reality', 'the primordial being', 'the highest being', 'the being of all beings', 'the thing in itself', or 'the sum-total of all possibilities'. 'God' is that single object which admits of all these descriptions. Kant refers technically to God as an 'ideal' insofar as this being is conceived of as an object, or concrete individual, akin to how the ideal of a perfectly wise person embodies the idea of wisdom. As such, God is the ideal object of pure reason.

Following the philosophical tradition, Kant recognizes only three basic ways to prove God's existence, and he argues that they all fail. One can start with pure concepts and aim through a definition of God, to prove God's existence in a rationalistic way. One can start empirically with some existent object and reason to God's existence from that object's contingency. Or, similarly, one can start with some determinate observations about the world, such as noting the order within it, and try to establish God's existence on that basis.

These approaches correspond to the three traditional arguments for God's existence in the history of philosophy, namely, the ontological argument, the cosmological argument and the teleological argument. The *ontological* argument is based on a definition of God and infers God's existence from the definition. The *cosmological* argument rests upon the observation that the world is filled with one or more contingently existing things, and infers God's existence from the need to explain the presence of such things. The *teleological* argument, which Kant calls the physico-theological argument, and which is also called the 'argument from design', stems from observing how the world is intelligently ordered, and infers God's existence from the presence of that order. With respect to these arguments, Kant writes:

> I shall show that neither on the one path, the empirical, nor on the other, the transcendental, can reason make progress [to God's existence], and that it stretches its wings in vain, if it tries to soar beyond the world of sense by the mere power of speculation.
>
> (A591/B619)

The ontological argument, popular among religiously oriented thinkers, is first within Kant's discussion. This argument defines God as the greatest, most perfect being, and infers that *as such*, 'existence' must be one of God's qualities. The reasoning is that if the greatest, most perfect being lacked any positive qualities, then it would not be absolutely perfect, so as an absolutely perfect being, it cannot lack in existence, which is a positive quality. We know that God exists by thinking carefully about what it means to be God.

Kant questions, though, whether it makes sense to refer to existence as a quality at all, let alone a positive or negative quality. Considering the definition of God and the question of whether or not God exists in relation to that definition, Kant argues that the logic of the situation requires that the meaning of the definition, or concept, of God remain stable as we consider whether the object of the concept, God, exists. To see this, let us ask whether there are one hundred dollars in Immanuel's pocket. Asking the question requires that we keep steadily in mind the concept, 'one hundred dollars in Immanuel's pocket', as we determine whether an object, the money, corresponds to the concept. Whether or not Immanuel happens to have the money, is a matter independent of the content of the concept, 'one hundred dollars in Immanuel's pocket'. This concept must be kept constant while we determine an answer to the question. If the money 'is' there in his pocket, this fact does not reflect back to affect the content of the concept, 'one hundred dollars in Immanuel's pocket'. As Kant explains it, the existence of the money does not (absurdly) increase the amount mentioned in the concept from one hundred, to say, one hundred and one. Adding 'existence' does not bear on the concept's content, and in the case of the definition of God, does not bear on God's perfection.

To reinforce this point, consider the concept of a 'broken down, malfunctioning old car'. If we add 'existence' to that concept, then it will not make the car any less broken down and malfunctioning, as if the additional existence could somehow 'repair' the car or make it 'better'. The same is true for the concept of a demonic being. If we add 'existence' to that concept, this will not render the demonic being any less demonic. Existence, then, is not a property, predicate or perfection, as the ontological argument requires. Even if one admits that existence is a property of some kind, contra Kant, existence could be neutral in value, or worse yet, negative. In some ancient myths we encounter the proposition that it is better not to be.

Key idea: Existence is not a predicate or property:
Suppose, as is usual, that some definition of an object provides us with a listing of the object's essential properties. Suppose we then ask whether the object exists. If the object happens to exist, or if it happens not to exist, the object's conceptual definition must remain constant throughout the inquiry. Otherwise, we would not be referring to the same object. Existence, then, cannot be on the list of any object's essential properties.

Kant does not believe that the ontological argument occurs naturally to people, and he regards it as an artificial product of scholastic philosophy. He is convinced that the argument was formulated as a supplement to the more fundamental and natural thought of wondering about the world, 'from where it all came'. Such is the spirit of the cosmological argument. We observe things in the world and realize for any one of them, or for the entire world, that it did not have to be there. We realize the world's contingency and ask therefore, how there could be anything at all, if there were not some necessary being at the universe's foundation. To avoid the absurdity that a contingent being or an infinitely long chain of contingent beings could be out of nowhere and for no reason, one supposes that there must be an absolutely necessary being, which is God.

Kant's immediate concern with the cosmological argument is in the last step, which equates an 'absolutely necessary being' with 'God', conceived of as 'the highest reality', 'supreme being', or 'most real' being. He denies that the thought of an absolutely necessary being implies a supreme being, since there is no contradiction in supposing that a limited being could be absolutely necessary. Polytheistic gods such as Zeus and Apollo, or Odin and Thor, could be examples.

If the cosmological argument is to succeed, the gap between 'absolutely necessary being' and 'supreme being', must be bridged. The argument starts with an existing contingent being and infers an existing absolutely necessary being. According to Kant, the only way to connect an absolutely necessary being with the more extensive thought of 'the highest reality', or 'supreme being' or 'being than which no greater can be conceived', is to argue conversely that the very idea of a supreme being implies the concept of an existing, absolutely necessary being. This, Kant observes, is none other than the ontological argument, which he has already shown to be invalid. He concludes that to reach a proper conception of God, the cosmological argument must rely on the ontological argument and consequently fails at least for that reason.

A more explicit, causally centred formulation of the cosmological argument more clearly illustrates Kant's point. Since a chain of causes and effects extends from the past into the present moment, and since each member of the chain is a contingent item, an 'uncaused' cause is required to begin the chain and make it possible. Suppose we accept this. The problem is that by itself, the concept of an uncaused cause is too thin for the argument's purposes, since it does not include the thought of being all-powerful, all-good, all-knowing or supreme.

The third traditional argument for God's existence is the teleological argument (or the argument from design), as it is usually known, or as Kant refers to it, the 'physico-theological' argument. He describes the argument's motivation inspiringly:

This present world presents to us so immeasurable a stage of variety, order, fitness, and beauty, whether we follow it up in the infinity of space or in its unlimited division, that even with the little knowledge which our poor understanding has been able to gather, all language, with regard to so many and inconceivable wonders, loses its vigour, all numbers their power of measuring, and all our thoughts their necessary determination; so that our judgement of the whole is lost in a speechless, but all the more eloquent astonishment...
(A622/B650)

The argument is that to account for the world's awesome regularity, there must be an intelligence that underlies the natural patterns, operating with great wisdom and a determinate purpose, which we call God. Contrasting with the respectful phrasing in which he presents it, Kant's estimation of the teleological argument is that it is the weakest of the three. At best, the argument establishes a world-designer, but not a world-creator, so it does not imply an all-sufficient, primordial being.

A stronger result can follow if the teleological argument is combined with the cosmological argument to introduce an absolutely necessary being as the intelligence-behind-the-scenes. At that point, though, the cosmological argument will still need to advance from an absolutely necessary being, albeit now endowed with intelligence, to a fully supreme being. For that, it must combine with the ontological argument.

In the end, Kant maintains that the teleological argument and the cosmological argument depend upon the ontological argument, and that the ontological argument is invalid, not to mention scholastically artificial. His sceptical position towards the traditional arguments for God's existence rests significantly on the weakness of the ontological argument, although each argument has a variety of other difficulties.

Key idea: The primacy of the ontological argument:

Kant claims that the teleological argument rests upon the cosmological argument, and that the cosmological argument rests upon the ontological argument. Arguing further that the ontological argument is invalid, Kant concludes that the teleological and cosmological arguments, like a house of cards, fall down together with the ontological argument.

As is true for the Paralogisms and Antinomy of Pure Reason, Kant extracts a constructive and consoling result from the failures of reason to obtain knowledge of what lies beyond the possibility of experience. Our reason generates the idea of God in its effort to know everything, but lacks the power to know whether a real being corresponds to that idea. That very idea of God nonetheless serves importantly and inevitably in the realm of appearances to guide regulatively, our inquiries in natural science.

Reason, as the intelligent supervisor and regulator for our scientific inquiries, dictates that we examine the world around us *as if* it were the product of a supreme intelligence. By expecting and looking for intelligent connections everywhere in our scientific endeavours, assuming that the world is coherently designed and purposeful through and through, we are led to discover more and more natural connections. In this way, by generating the concept of God as the intelligent designer of the world, reason guides us towards achieving the greatest unity combined with the greatest detail in our *scientific* knowledge of the world. Not only, then, does reason have a practical application in the moral sphere of what we ought to do, it pragmatically aids science, which intends thoroughly to understand the mechanical and factual details of experience.

Dig Deeper

Sadik J. Al-Azm, *The Origins of Kant's Arguments in the Antinomies* (Clarendon Press, 1972)

Michelle Grier, *Kant's Doctrine of Transcendental Illusion*, Chapters 6 and 7 (Cambridge University Press, 2001)

Christopher David Shaw, *On Exceeding Determination and the Ideal of Reason* (Cambridge Scholars Publishing, 2012)

Victoria S. Wike, *Kant's Antinomies of Reason* (University Press of America, 1982)

Allen Wood, *Kant's Rational Theology* (Cornell University Press, 1978)

Study questions

1 What are the four main philosophical questions in the Antinomy of Pure Reason?

2 Why does Kant believe that it makes no sense to ask whether or not the world had a beginning?

3 Why does Kant believe that there need be no contradiction in asserting that we are both free and not free?

4 Which of the three traditional arguments for God's existence does Kant believe is the weakest?

5 Which of the three traditional arguments for God's existence does Kant believe is the most natural and expressive of a fundamental human puzzlement?

6 Which of the three traditional arguments for God's existence does Kant believe is the most artificial?

7 What is the difference between an 'absolutely necessary being' and a 'supreme being'?

8 Of the three traditional arguments for God's existence, upon which of the three arguments does Kant believe the other two rest?

9 With respect to the ontological argument, what does it mean to say that existence is not a 'property' or 'perfection'?

10 What consolations does Kant offer at the ends of the Antinomies and the Ideal of Reason that offset his more sceptical analyses?

Section Three:

What should we do?

10

Freedom and moral awareness

Morality presupposes freedom. To hold a person morally responsible for some action, is to assume that the person is free. This chapter describes how Kant defines freedom as being independent of our worldly, sensuous desires and personal happiness. Modelled upon a conception of God's timeless activity, Kant characterizes freedom independently of the spatio-temporal world, thereby locating it metaphysically closer to ultimate reality. Despite the natural world's mechanical operations, Kant maintains as a hallmark of his outlook that freedom is compatible with nature, for what we experience as nature is only the mere appearance of ultimate reality.

Kant's second *Critique*, the *Critique of Practical Reason* (*CPrR*), establishes the foundation of his moral theory in the concept of freedom. Its subject is 'practical' reason, which Kant distinguishes sharply from 'speculative' reason, the focus of the first *Critique*. Speculative reason is reason's employment in the quest for metaphysical knowledge, as it tries to extend the categories of the understanding into a realm beyond the possibility of human experience. In the *Critique of Pure Reason*, as we know, Kant shows that while remaining powerless to determine the metaphysical source of either the world or our ultimate inner being, reason supplies the ideal of integrating our day-to-day factual knowledge into a complete scientific system. When Kant uses the word 'speculation', he accordingly signifies the denial of metaphysical knowledge and affirmation of its regulative function as the systematizer of scientific knowledge.

For Kant, reason's inability to answer metaphysical questions has it benefits. Rather than remaining in benighted bondage to pointless speculation and the endless conflict of opinion, recognizing the limits of reason redirects our attention liberatingly and peacefully to the world of daily affairs with the assurance that as 'practical' reason, we remain in possession of solid moral guidance. Independently of experience, reason can determine what we ought to do, and even more generally, how the world ought to be.

As a causal power that can 'bring forth objects corresponding to conceptions' (*CPrR*, Introduction), reason is intelligently creative. Accompanying this creativity is a vision of what the world would be like, if reason, like a perfect sovereign, were to govern the world entirely, operating in perfect harmony with the laws of nature. Kant envisions that if only everyone were to act in accord with reason's moral dictates, respecting the divine voice within us, an earthly Kingdom of God would result, filled with mutually respecting people.

This all sounds metaphysical, idealized, and certainly religious, but practical reason officially makes no metaphysical claims. Kant grounds these visions upon the simple recognition – the 'moral fact' – that moral considerations are independent of both gratifying sensory pleasure and threatening pain. The following passage is both memorable and illustrative:

> *Suppose someone asserts of his lustful appetite that, when the desired object and the opportunity are present, it is quite irresistible. Ask him, though, if a gallows were erected next to the place where he finds this opportunity, in order that he should be hanged immediately after the gratification of his lust, whether he could not then control his passion. We need not wait long in doubt about what he would reply. Ask him, however, if his sovereign ordered him, on pain of the same immediate execution, to bear false witness against an honourable man, whom the prince might wish to destroy under a plausible pretext, whether he would consider it possible in that case to overcome his love of life, however great it may be. He would perhaps not venture to affirm whether he would do so or not, but he must unhesitatingly admit that it is possible to do so. He judges, therefore, that he can do a certain thing because he is conscious that he ought, and he recognizes that he is free – a fact which but for the moral law he would never have known.*
>
> (CPrR, Section 6)

Such examples inform Kant's conviction that our moral awareness is independent of, and not subservient to, sensory pleasures, gratifications, attractions, satisfactions and the like. To him, it is misguided to believe that the purpose of morality is to maximize the pleasure in the world, where 'good' essentially means 'pleasure' and 'evil' essentially means 'pain'. That for the sake of upholding justice and respect for other people, we are willing to forsake the most gratifying sensory pleasures and even sacrifice our lives, is evidence to Kant that to understand the source of morality, we must set our sights beyond the sensory world, with its attendant pleasures and pains.

This coheres well with Kant's abstractive philosophical method, and he develops a position that locates the source of morality in our reason, independently of experience. Just as he identifies the *a priori* foundations of human knowledge in the forms of space and time in conjunction with the conceptual forms of the understanding, regarded as empty of sensory content, he identifies the *a priori* source of morality in yet another sensation-independent form, as we shall see more specifically in the next chapter.

Insofar as these various forms are independent of experience, their *a priori* nature lends them a universality and necessity that *dignifies* them above the changing sensory scenes. We speak here of a moral theory which purports to be strong, steadfast and applicable to all rational beings. Kant's theory of beauty – also a subject for later chapters – rests equally and analogously upon disregarding an object's gratifying sensory qualities (which he calls 'charm') to highlight the object's universally appreciable spatio-temporal structure, in part for the sake of reinforcing moral awareness.

It is frequently assumed that morality's aim is to bring happiness into the world, not merely for oneself, but for everyone. There are many conceptions of happiness, but in Kant, 'happiness' refers to the overall satisfaction of one's worldly desires. In his words, 'happiness is the condition of a rational being in the world, with whom everything goes according to his wish and will' (*CPrR*, Book II, Chapter II, Section V).

He sees, however, an insurmountable problem with grounding morality upon happiness: people want different things, so there are no universally applicable rules that can fulfill everyone's desire without conflict. Worse yet, when people desire the same thing – for example, land with food and energy sources – there is often a fight to possess it, sometimes vicious. Rather than being intrinsically moral, the single-minded quest for happiness tends rather to produce the 'most angry conflict' (*CPrR*, Section 4). Happiness may be desirable for individuals in a worldly sense, but Kant regards happiness as an appendage to morality: if one acts morally, then one deserves to be happy.

Spotlight: Kant's moral theory in perspective

According to Kant, an action has moral value if it issues from a good will, motivated purely out of respect for duty and the moral law. The action's consequences are secondary. The word for 'duty' or 'obligation' in ancient Greek is *deon*, and Kant's non-consequentialist moral theory is accordingly called a 'deontological' theory. Other moral theories – the 'consequentialist' theories, of which utilitarianism is an example – determine an action's moral value in reference to its consequences: if the consequences promote whatever is considered to be good, then the action is moral.

Neither kind of theory is perfect. By always telling the truth out of a respect for duty, hurt feelings and needless suffering can result. If done with cold calculation, killing one person to save five is not clearly moral, despite the consequences.

There are yet other moral theories, aiming to be more realistic and practical, which emphasize the development of good character and virtue. These theories in the field of 'virtue ethics' appeal to paradigms of good character and to desirable arrays of character traits to be fostered. The inherent flexibility of such examples and idealized constructions, subject to empirical contingencies as they are, remains, however, a matter for debate.

Having established that the foundation of morality is independent of the sensory world of space, time, animal desires and ordinary survival, Kant asks characteristically, 'What, fundamentally, does our moral awareness presuppose?' His answer is that it requires the power to choose. Consider another revealing passage:

> There are cases in which men, even with the same education which has been profitable to others, yet show such early depravity, and so continue to progress in it to years of manhood, that they are thought to be born villains, and their character altogether incapable of improvement; and nevertheless they are judged for what they do or leave undone, they are reproached for their faults as guilty; nay, they themselves regard these reproaches as well founded, exactly as if in spite of the hopeless natural quality of mind ascribed to them, they remained just as responsible as any other man.
> (CPrR, Book I, Chapter III, Critical Elucidation)

As a condition for moral awareness and the accompanying ascriptions of praise and blame, one must suppose that each person is free. Only with this assumption does it make sense to say of a person that he or she could have done otherwise. This brings us to Kant's theory of freedom, and to how it works within the conclusions of the *Critique of Pure Reason*.

Key idea: Moral awareness is independent of sensory pleasures and happiness:

Since the spatio-temporal world operates mechanistically and deterministically, Kant locates our freedom and the basis of morality beyond space and time. From the moral standpoint, this renders as a merely secondary concern, our happiness as the fulfilment of worldly desires.

In the first *Critique*, the Third Antinomy maintains that although freedom cannot be proven in a mathematical, logical or scientific sense, if we uphold the distinction between how things appear and how things are in themselves, then freedom is possible. If, to the contrary, the physical world were the world of things in themselves, then there would be no freedom, for like an ever-ticking clockwork, the physical world would be the only world, deterministic and thoroughly understandable by natural science. Upon recognizing that the mechanically operating, spatio-temporal world is merely an appearance, freedom becomes possible outside of and independently of that world. As such, it is spaceless and timeless.

This yields a 'double-aspect' theory, structured like the two sides of a coin, where from the perspective of how things appear, we are unfree, physically determined beings, and from the perspective of how things are in themselves, we are free agents whose essence is not of the spatio-temporal world. We cannot know substantially what we ultimately are, but the fact of our moral awareness implies that we are essentially free. In light of this moral awareness, we must 'postulate' freedom.

Despite its weaker cognitive status as a postulate of practical reason, as opposed to being a matter of proven knowledge, freedom is paramount in Kant's philosophy. Indeed he states: 'the concept of freedom, inasmuch as its reality is proved by an apodeictic law of practical reason, it is the keystone of the whole edifice of pure reason, and even of speculative reason' (*CPrR*, Preface). With this wider glimpse of Kant's philosophy, we can say that practical reason contains the deeper significance of pure reason.

Kant's concept of freedom nonetheless introduces some mystery. In the *Critique of Pure Reason*, he conceives of human freedom on the model of how God, operating independently of space and time, created the world 'spontaneously' (A533/B561). Although religiously moving, this way of understanding freedom generates a series of puzzling assertions that describe our personal character (our 'intelligible character' or 'timelessly true character') in its condition as a free agent. For instance, Kant states that in our intelligible character 'no *action* would *begin* or *cease*' (A540/B568) and that 'inasmuch as it is *noumenon*, nothing *happens* in it' (A541/B569). He adds that 'as a purely intelligible faculty, pure reason is not subject to the form of time, nor consequently to the conditions of succession in time' (A551/B579) and that 'the causality of reason in its intelligible character, in producing an effect, does *not arise* or begin to be at a certain time' (A551/B579).

These quotes present a theory of 'timeless agency', where, as a condition for moral awareness, we must consider ourselves to be timeless beings in reality, where our free actions are echoes of God's creation of the universe. The Biblical idea that humans are made in God's image resonates loudly throughout Kant's theory of freedom. The doctrine remains mysterious insofar as it is difficult to comprehend how any being, God or human, can *act* independently of time.

We can nevertheless appreciate Kant as holding generally that our ultimate inner being determines how we appear in space and time. A person makes many decisions across a lifetime, and these can be understood together as the accumulated expressions of the person's constant, intelligible character. If a person cheats when playing games as a young child, then as an adult, we can expect that person to cheat when playing for advantage in the workplace; if a person shows compassion for animals when young, then as an adult, we can expect to see the same compassion. Just as different patches of blue express the same timeless idea of blueness, a person's variety of actions over time express his or her timeless character. Someone's intelligible character can also be imagined as being complicated, allowing for apparent changes in behaviour over time.

This kind of theory would not have us blame a person on a case-by-case basis, for having done this or that at such-and-such a time. We would instead think more generally, and blame the person for being the kind of character he or she is. Notwithstanding how this view modifies our usual way of thinking, Kant's overall point is that if we distinguish between things in themselves and their appearances, then freedom and determinism are compatible. With such a distinction in hand, it becomes possible to understand morality as involving absolute commands and as prescribing a determinate vision of how the world ought to be.

As noted, Kant associates happiness with the overall satisfaction of worldly desires. As a phenomenon in the sensory world of space and time, however, happiness is not ultimately real. By accepting this, and upon denying accordingly that happiness is the guidelight for morality, the otherworldly nature of freedom becomes salient. To foster moral awareness, we need to conceive of ourselves as being independent of sensory pleasures and material things, aligning what we are in truth with a more dignified level of being. Kant sums it up nicely: 'in the doctrine of happiness empirical principles constitute the entire foundation, but in the doctrine of morality they do not form the smallest part of it' (*CPrR*, Book I, Chapter III, Critical Elucidation).

We should observe in passing that the moral law, insofar as it is independent of happiness, can be hard: it does not necessarily cohere with our natural inclinations and animal desires. When acted upon, it can *constrain* our desire, resulting in pain and frustration. Since cultivating moral awareness requires control over and detachment from the desire for sensory gratification, it can be useful in the larger picture to recall the ancient wisdom that desire itself can lead existentially to frustration and emptiness, and that distancing oneself from desire can be morally beneficial as a safeguard against feelings of meaninglessness.

Kant's prescriptions never go this far, as he more temperately anticipates a world that ultimately synchronizes morality and happiness. A more ascetic outlook can nonetheless serve well for appreciating the import and tenor of Kant's moral theory, even though he does not portray sensuous desire as negatively as the Buddhists and Hindus, remaining content simply to diminish its value by squarely subordinating it to reason. As far as he can see, though, it stands to reason that curbing one's sensuality is tantamount to preserving one's dignity.

Dig Deeper

Henry Allison, *Kant's Theory of Freedom* (Cambridge University Press, 1990)

Lewis White Beck, *A Commentary on Kant's Critique of Practical Reason* (University of Chicago Press, 1960)

Hud Hudson, *Kant's Compatibilism* (Cornell University Press, 1994)

Christopher J. Insole, *Kant and the Creation of Freedom: A Theological Problem* (Oxford University Press, 2013)

Richard McCarty, *Kant's Theory of Action* (Oxford University Press, 2009)

Richard Velkley, *Freedom and the Ends of Reason: On the Moral Foundations of Kant's Critical Philosophy* (University of Chicago Press, 1989)

Study questions

1 What is the difference between speculative reason and practical reason?

2 Upon what fact does Kant maintain that we are free agents?

3 For freedom to be possible, why must one deny that the spatio-temporal world is the single, ultimately real world?

4 Why does Kant believe that the goal of morality is not to produce happiness in the world?

5 What is the difference between a deontological moral theory and a consequentialist moral theory?

6 How does Kant's 'double-aspect' theory of reality render freedom and determinism compatible?

7 Upon what model does Kant develop a conception of human freedom?

8 What is a person's 'intelligible character'?

9 What is meant by 'timeless agency'?

10 What is the contrast between dignity and sensuosity?

11

The morality of self-respect

Kant's moral theory is both rationalistic and universalistic: it determines moral value in reference to an action's reasonableness, and it intends to apply to all rational beings. One's sense of duty and having a good will become thereby a matter of respect for oneself as a rational being. In this chapter we will see how Kant's moral theory is based on the very idea of law, and how the respect for law is expressed in the absolute moral command to act consistently, known as the 'categorical imperative'.

1 Duty and the moral law

There are many facts about the world – those regarding its colours, tastes and sounds, for instance – which might have been different. The boiling and freezing temperatures of water might have been higher, humans might naturally have had the capacity to see radio waves and microwaves, the overall amounts of pleasures and pains in the world might have been otherwise distributed, the average kinds of emotional reactions to situations might have been less or more intense, the earth might have had three moons, Jesus, Buddha, Mohammad, Napoleon and Hitler might never have been born, and so on. The world is filled with contingencies and it appears the way it does largely because of those contingencies.

Throughout these variations and possibilities, it remains constant that all human experience must occur in time and that $2 + 2 = 4$. Kant's philosophy in general, attracted by such constancies in the recognition of how stability follows from truth, aims for knowledge that is *not* subject to contingencies, as it seeks what is universal and necessary, discovering it in what is knowable *a priori*. Kant's moral theory is no exception.

Observing how the respect for other people and the moral law can overcome the love for life itself, Kant infers that our moral awareness is independent of contingent sensory pleasures and pains, and that worldly happiness is a tangential matter. Morality, he maintains, resides in our better half, issuing from our reason and inherent freedom.

Central to Kant's moral theory is accordingly the distinction between the sensory world of contingencies and the intelligible world of constant realities. As appearances in space and time, our animal qualities have their place and function, but as timeless realities beyond space and time, our freedom and reason reflect our true nature. The world's contingencies and the happiness they can provide are mere appearances. Our moral awareness implies that we are essentially beings dignified beyond these appearances.

As independent of the sensory world, Kant conceives of our will's goodness as the allegiance to do what is right, whatever the worldly consequences may be. It is easy to assume otherwise that a good will concerns having virtues such as courage, intelligence and perseverance, but having a set of virtues does not imply being good. An evil person could have the same set, and use the virtues as instruments, selfishly, hurtfully and destructively. With extraordinary courage, intelligence and perseverance, a criminal would be that much more dangerous. Moreover, given the material destitution of many saints, it is also unconvincing classically to characterize good people and their wills, in reference to worldly success, power, and health.

For Kant, to appreciate the foundation of our moral awareness and the nature of a good will requires an exclusive attention to the quality of a person's inner being, apart from sensory interests and inclinations. This independence from spatio-temporal appearances is central, for Kant is most impressed by our capacity not to be swayed by physical considerations when faced with hard moral choices. Recall the example of a person who, when mortally threatened by state authorities to bear false and deadly witness against an innocent neighbour, stands up defiantly to the despicable intimidation.

Upholding one of the Ten Commandments without qualification, as we see in this example, displays how acting purely out of respect for the moral law can be stronger than life itself. For Kant, the example confirms that the moral law is not grounded in the changing and contingent world, but stems from reality, in reason and freedom. Our reason commands *respect* in its power to withstand the most extreme pressure from the worldly 'carrot and the stick', which frequently takes the form of bribes and physical threats.

Acting exclusively out of respect for the moral law is to act from a sense of *duty*, acknowledging our finite and fallible condition in the ordinary world. Since the moral law is a function of our reason, expressive of our intelligible, non-sensory being, acting from a sense of duty is to act from a *feeling of respect* for our better, intelligible self. Morality is about respecting this intelligible aspect more than our animal aspect, knowing how the latter's interests and inclinations reside in the world of pleasures and pains, a mere world of appearances and contingencies.

Key idea: Moral awareness is self-respect for ourselves as rational beings:

Kant maintains that we are essentially rational beings, so as a matter of respect towards ourselves as such, we ought to act consistently. Our feeling of dignity or self-respect as rational beings yields a sense of duty and is the basis of a good will.

To appreciate further the spirit of Kant's moral theory, it helps to remember how in the first *Critique*, the accounts of space and time in the Transcendental Aesthetic are based upon a process of abstraction. Starting with any ordinary object, Kant imaginatively sets aside the object's sensory qualities and concept of the object's kind to highlight for exclusive attention, the object's spatio-temporal form that remains. Space and time consequently present themselves as empty containers, independent of any sensory content that experience might fillingly provide. Similarly in the Transcendental Logic, Kant conceives of the concepts of the understanding as pure, empty forms that organize given sensory inputs.

In his moral theory, Kant uses the same kind of approach, as he judges the moral value of actions in abstraction from sensory gratifications, pains, and happiness. Where this process of abstraction leads is surprising, since at first, it is difficult to imagine how the resulting principle can serve as the basis for morality.

Prior to the *Critique of Practical Reason*, which we discussed in the last chapter, Kant published a preliminary work on morality – a 'groundwork' or 'foundation' as he called it – three years earlier in 1785. This book, the *Groundwork of the Metaphysics of Morals*, appearing four years after the publication of the first edition of the *Critique of Pure Reason*, stands well as an introduction to Kant's moral theory. Although he does not develop the theory of freedom to the informative extent as he does in the second *Critique*, leaving the ultimate basis of morality to await further elaboration, the *Groundwork* (also called the *Foundations of the Metaphysics of Morals*), describes the meaning of acting from duty in solid and useful detail.

As we know, the *Critique of Pure Reason* tells us how reason systematizes that towards which it is directed. It systematizes the understanding and the empirical knowledge subsumed under the understanding. It also strives for totality, searching for closure in the causal series of spatio-temporal events, and precipitating thereby the ideas of freedom, soul and world. Reason aims to systematize everything. Since there can be no system of any kind without some fixed rules, principles, or laws that give the system its structure – and here is the key idea – at the basis of reason is *the concept of law itself*, pure and simple.

To respect ourselves as rational beings amounts to respecting unconditionally the very thought of law itself. *This*, according to Kant, is the basis of morality. A good will acts exclusively out of the respect for law itself. Accordingly, acting morally is to act with no other motivation in view but the respect for law. There are no specific 'laws' of morality at the foundation of morality. These come later. Acting morally is to act generally out of respect for ourselves as rational, and hence as law-formulating, legislating beings. Such self-respect implies that we act independently of sensuous interests and personal inclinations, for these have nothing to do with, and are indeed subject to, what we timelessly are as law-giving beings.

Key idea: 'Acting merely in accord with what duty requires' as opposed to 'acting because duty requires it':

Merely out of self-interest, a shopkeeper might act honestly in all instances, realizing that the public appearance of honesty will increase profits. A different shopkeeper might act honestly in all instances exclusively from a sense of duty, or self-respect as a rational being. Although the external behaviours might be identical in both cases, Kant maintains that the selfishly-motivated shopkeeper's actions have no moral worth, whereas the self-respecting shopkeeper's actions are morally praiseworthy.

This may all sound reasonable, if a bit out of the ordinary, but one might still wonder how the mere respect for ourselves as law-giving beings – that is, how the sheer respect for law itself – can provide any specific moral directives. The concept of 'law itself' seems too thin to ground an entire moral theory.

Kant's thought is this: when deciding what we ought to do, we should never act in a way that undermines the concept of law, which is at the core of our intelligible character. This means that we always ought to act *consistently*. It also means that we should act 'as a human being', not primarily as John or Mary, or as a member of some national, religious, political, sports, tribal, or other social group whose definition imposes a less enlightened mentality of 'us versus them'. Acting morally requires that we consider ourselves first and foremost as 'human beings' – and indeed more precisely and generally as 'rational beings' – equally and together on a level playing field, acting not in view of our animal nature, but in view of, and with respect for, our intelligible, free, law-giving, rational being.

Spotlight: Moral feelings: Kant and Hume

Kant's moral theory is often contrasted with that of David Hume, who believed that morality is not founded upon reason, but upon natural feelings or sentiments. One of Hume's more well-known remarks – 'reason is the slave of the passions' – sets him clearly in opposition to Kant. Hume writes:

> *An action, or sentiment, or character is virtuous or vicious; why? Because its view causes a pleasure or uneasiness of a particular kind. In giving a reason, therefore, for the pleasure or uneasiness, we sufficiently explain the vice or virtue. To have the sense of virtue, is nothing but to feel a satisfaction of a particular kind from the contemplation of a character. The very feeling constitutes our praise or admiration. We go no farther; nor do we enquire into the cause of the satisfaction. (Treatise on Human Nature, Book III, Section II)*

Such remarks can suggest easily that the crucial difference between Kant's ethics and Hume's ethics, is that Hume's is based on 'feelings', whereas Kant's view is based on reason, and not feelings. A better way to draw the contrast, though, is to say that both views are based on feelings, but upon feelings of very different kinds. Kant's view is based on a unique, unconditional, *non-sensory* feeling of respect for ourselves as rational beings, knowable *a priori*, whereas Hume's view is based on *sensory* feelings, empirical, contingent, and knowable only *a posteriori*.

2 The categorical imperative

When we act, there is the specific action and also a way to interpret that action. The interpretation allows us to think about the action in a more general way, with a measure of rationality. Considering the action's rationality *per se* involves thinking about it in light of a rule, in relation to which the action is an example. Suppose on some occasion, for instance, the action is to tell a lie as the only way to escape some embarrassment. We can express the action's rationality in reference to how it falls under a rule that one is implicitly following.

What, then, could be the rule in this case? It could be formulated as 'in any situation where I can escape embarrassment only by telling a lie, then I will tell the lie'. This is the 'maxim' that is being followed. For any action at all, then, there is some maxim that one is implicitly following that lends the action some rationality. At the personal level at which the maxim is now being formulated, it refers only to 'me' and to what 'I' would do, so the rationality involved is fairly minimal insofar as the wider context of society at large is not being brought into account. Still, we are appreciating the action as falling under a rule with a measure of rationality, as opposed to considering it as an isolated, singular, uninterpreted occurrence.

With respect to determining an action's moral value, Kant's question is simple: does the maxim of my action make sense in reference to me as a *rational being in general*? At this point, we are no longer thinking of the maxim merely in reference to 'me' as a single individual, but to 'me' in a wider, truer sense, as an equal member of humanity as a whole and as a rational being. If the more broadly formulated, more inclusive maxim does not make sense, and if we perform the action nonetheless, then we are being irrational, and are disrespecting ourselves as rational beings. To do this would be to act neither from duty nor from a good will, but immorally.

Let us, then, consider the rationality of the generalized maxim in our example: 'in any situation where one (i.e., anyone) can escape embarrassment only by telling a lie, then tell the lie'. Since we are considering the action from the standpoint of being a human in general, the maxim is potentially a rule that everyone would be following. It could be formulated as: 'for any human being, in any situation where one can escape embarrassment only by telling a lie, then tell the lie'. Does it still make sense at this level of generalization?

It is intriguing to see that once this maxim is generalized, it self-destructs. Once everyone consequently assumes that anyone to whom they are speaking is likely to be lying, 'lying' *per se* would be impossible. Since telling a lie involves presenting a falsehood as a truth, no lies can be told if, at the outset, no one expects that the truth is being told. Once the maxim about lying under pressure is generalized across all contexts and people, deception becomes impossible and telling lies no longer makes sense. The situation compares to how, once it becomes common knowledge that a social organization has been continually lying to the people, the organization's 'true' pronouncements no longer count as having any *prima facie* truth.

Since the generalized maxim falls apart, it is a non-entity that no one can adopt. In view of the maxim's irrationality, Kant concludes that lying under duress is immoral. The formula for this style of decision making and moral assessment, and Kant's consequent expression of the unconditional moral directive associated with it, is as follows:

Act only according to that maxim whereby you can at the same time will that it should become a universal law.
(Groundwork, Second Section)

Kant refers to this as the 'categorical' imperative. It is an absolute command that issues from our being rational. The imperative's necessity compares to that of the categories of the understanding, insofar as the latter issue from our being logical. We carry the categorical imperative and the categories of the understanding into worldly experience as an expression of what we essentially are. In this regard, the categorical imperative is not optional or conditional. For us, it is unconditional, for it does not say conditionally that 'if' we happen to want such-and-such, 'then' we should do this or that to obtain it. It is not a 'hypothetical imperative'. As an expression of our inner being, the categorical imperative is 'necessary' for us and is knowable *a priori*.

The conclusion of the *Critique of Practical Reason* begins with the often-quoted remark that 'two things fill the mind with ever new and increasing admiration and awe, the more often and more steadily we reflect on them: the starry heavens above me and the moral law within me'. Kant is here conceiving of two, fully developed systems of law, natural law and moral law. He realizes that our moral activity shows its effects in the spatio-temporal world wherein natural law determines all events, so the universalized maxims that we adopt for moral activity must be compatible with natural law.

Our reason, located independently of the spatio-temporal world, imposes upon us as spatio-temporal beings, the obligation to act in a consistent way. Since it is irrational to conceive of reason itself as being irrational, reason can obligate us to act in such-and-such a way within the spatio-temporal world only if it is *possible* for us to act in such a way. 'Ought' implies 'can'. If so, then the moral law must cohere with the natural law.

To express the compatibility between morality and nature, Kant offers a second formulation of the categorical imperative, much like the first, which is to 'act as though the maxim of your action were to become by your will, a universal law of nature' (*Groundwork*, Second Section). This calls up the image of everyone in the world acting in social harmony, akin to how the planets and celestial bodies move together in harmony within the natural system of the physical universe. 'Activity according to law' is the idea shared by two systems of law, moral and physical.

Since acting from duty alone is a matter of acting out of respect for oneself as a rational, law-giving being, having a good will is having self-respect as a free human being. Given this tight connection between duty and self-respect, yet another way to express the categorical imperative is to require that we always respect the humanity in ourselves and in everyone else. This yields a third formulation of the categorical imperative, expressive of the dignity of the human being: 'act so that you treat humanity, whether in your own person or in that of another, in every case as an end and never as a means only' (*Groundwork*, Second Section).

These three formulations of the categorical imperative provide alternative, but as Kant intends, equivalent, ways to conceptualize the morality of various actions. The third formulation is perhaps the most intuitive, easiest to grasp and apply, as it prescribes that out of respect for ourselves and others, for instance, we honour our parents and other people, that we do not murder, steal, or lie, and that we refrain from abusing ourselves.

Key idea: The categorical imperative:

This is the unconditional moral command to act consistently. It differs from merely pragmatic or 'hypothetical' directives which prescribe that 'if' one wants such and such, 'then' do this or that. Unlike hypothetical imperatives, the categorical imperative is a steadfast expression of the respect for law itself.

Kant's overall approach to morality – one which is grounded in the single principle of respecting the concept of law, independently of the sensuous, spatio-temporal world – further instructs us not to confuse this single principle of morality with sensuous imagery and other principles that mistakenly purport to express the true morality, such as worldly happiness. Echoing the first of the Ten Commandments, which prescribes that we recognize 'no other gods', we can see in Kant's insistence that the categorical imperative is the sole determinant of moral value, that his moral theory, in conjunction with the above comments and examples, can be appreciated as having been inspired by the Ten Commandments, whose foundation he is rethinking carefully at the height of intellectual sophistication, abstraction and refinement.

No theory is perfect, and Kant's moral theory has some difficulties to resolve. First of all, when applying the categorical imperative to actual situations, the maxim of the action in question needs to be formulated with some reasonable honesty. Consider the maxim above concerning lying under duress. It is easy to escape responsibility by formulating the maxim narrowly such as 'for any human being, and for any situation in this room at noon on 8 July 1947, where one can escape embarrassment only by telling a lie, then tell the lie'.

If interpreted within the narrow circumstances described, the maxim may still fall apart, since no one in the room could reasonably will the maxim, but if the maxim is more extensively situated within an ordinary-world context, where telling the truth remains common practice, the maxim's generalization will not have any widespread effect on the meaning of truth-telling. The exact level at which we should formulate any particular maxim is consequently unclear, as is how we should characterize the measure of honesty and wisdom required to formulate it responsibly.

In addition to the case of lying under duress, Kant applies the categorical imperative to conclude that we should not commit suicide, that we should develop our talents, and that we should help other people in distress. If we accept these prescriptions, even admitting that the latter two duties are less pressing, it can be difficult to see how to formulate the maxims of one's actions when the prescriptions come into conflict.

On certain occasions – and Kant offers some of these examples himself – one might decide to commit suicide to defend one's country, as did the Japanese kamikaze pilots during World War II, or to commit suicide in the face of an agonizing death from disease. Similarly, one might decide to perpetuate a lie by respecting the orders of a governmental or military superior, aware that the lie's effectiveness will cause many innocent people to die. Less intensely, one might need to tell lies to secure the best opportunity to develop one's talents, or one might find developing one's talents to be so demanding, that it requires the serious neglect of other people's needs. It is a challenge to resolve these conflict-filled situations through an application of the categorical imperative alone.

Objections to Kant's moral theory also arise from those who find that excluding love and compassion from the determination of moral value is inconsistent with ordinary practice. Others maintain that the categorical imperative, at least in its first formulation, is an unrealistic abstraction, since no one ever uses it when making moral decisions and assessments. Still others find it difficult to accept that we should set aside the consequences of a person's action when determining its moral value, discerning, for instance, a significant moral difference – one that the law and common opinion recognizes – between attempted murder and actual murder.

Dig Deeper

Marcia Baron, *Kantian Ethics Almost Without Apology* (Cornell University Press, 1995)

Paul Guyer, *Kant on Freedom, Law and Happiness* (Cambridge University Press, 2000)

Onora O'Neill, *Constructions of Reason: Explorations of Kant's Practical Philosophy* (Cambridge University Press, 1989)

Jens Timmerman, *Kant's 'Groundwork of the Metaphysics of Morals': A Critical Guide* (Cambridge University Press, 2013)

Allen Wood, *Kant's Ethical Thought* (Cambridge University Press, 1999)

Study questions

1 Why is having a set of virtues or being wealthy not sufficient for having a good will?

2 How can morality be based on the mere concept of law itself?

3 What is the difference between acting from duty and acting merely in accord with duty?

4 What does it mean for an imperative to be 'categorical', as opposed to 'hypothetical'?

5 To determine whether an action is morally permissible, why do we need to generalize the maxim of the action?

6 How are the Ten Commandments related to the categorical imperative?

7 In Kant's moral theory, how are rationality, morality, duty and self-respect interrelated?

8 Three different formulations of the categorical imperative were mentioned. How are these related to each other?

9 How does the phrase 'ought implies can' concern the harmony of nature and morality?

10 What are four objections to Kant's moral theory?

12

God, virtue and evil

Kant's moral theory culminates in a vision of society where everyone acts from a sense of duty and is awarded happiness to realize the highest good. This chapter outlines Kant's idealized social vision, explaining how it is founded upon the three postulates of practical reason: freedom, immortality of the soul, and the existence of God. The chapter concludes with a discussion of the problem of evil as expressed through the Book of Job. We will see that Kant's moral theory accounts for the source of Job's unyielding faith and sense of personal dignity in the face of crushing personal hardship, and provides a practical attitude towards the presence of evil in the world.

1 The 'realm of ends' and the highest good

It may sound self-evident to say that throughout Kant's philosophy, human experience is interpreted exclusively from the standpoint of being human. Our experience, however, can be interpreted from a variety of standpoints. We might ask instead of some situation, 'Is it good for our family?', 'Is it good for our nation?', 'Is it good for our religion?', 'Is it good for our corporation?', 'Is it good for my career?', and so on. In contrast to these more restricted standpoints, thinking universally and exclusively 'as a human being' is relatively uncommon. It takes an especially broad-minded person to set aside considerations such as family, nation, religion and workplace to act and interpret the world exclusively as a human being *per se*.

Speaking as a human being in general, Kant describes in his theory of knowledge how all possible human experience must occur as a set of causally connected objects in space and time. Also speaking for everyone in his moral theory, he argues how we should consider our moral actions as being performed exclusively by the 'humanity' within us. This perspective reveals a strong social dimension to Kant's philosophy. To universalize successfully the maxim of one's action in accord with the categorical imperative, is for the humanity within us to legislate for humanity as a whole, and to view our actions in relation to billions of people in a great, systematic community. Kant describes the situation in the following:

> ...*every rational being must act as if, by his maxims, he were in every case a legislating member in the universal kingdom of ends. The formal principle of these maxims is: So act as if thy maxim were to serve likewise as the universal law (of all rational beings).*
>
> (Groundwork, Second Section)

Insofar as each of us is a timelessly free, autonomous, rational and self-respecting agent, to be treated never as a means only but always also as an end in itself, our activity participates in a 'realm' (*Reich*) of ends, or moral social system. This realm of ends is an abstraction. It is an idealized community of people, all of whom act morally, and all of whom thereby deserve happiness. Notwithstanding its status as an idealization, since within this realm everyone acts only from duty, happiness is not a necessary part of the realm of ends.

In English translations of Kant's writings, the realm of ends is sometimes called the 'kingdom of ends', but there is no 'king' or monarchy involved. If described in phrasings from political philosophy, each person is a 'legislative member' in this realm and reason itself is the sovereign, embodied equally and throughout the inner being of its citizenship. The laws within the realm therefore express the rational will of the community as a whole. Within this world of purified humanity, one acts as part of an ideal society where the laws are instituted according to everyone's single and univocal voice, and where every person consequently follows human dictates and is in that sense, free.

The duty to turn this idealized moral realm into a reality requires Kant to reintroduce some central ideas from the Dialectic of Pure Reason in the first *Critique*. Since reason requires that we act from duty and prescribes an ideal moral condition wherein all of our actions issue from a respect for duty, Kant asks whether to realize this realm of perfected humanity, we need to suppose anything further. We know that morality presupposes that we are free. To cultivate oneself morally to the point where actions are *always* done from duty, with a virtually holy attitude, however, requires some time. Indeed, Kant believes that it requires infinite time, so to complete morality's demands, he maintains that we must postulate the soul's immortality, 'an endless duration of the existence and personality of the same rational being' (*Critique of Practical Reason*, Book II, Chapter II, Section IV).

We are familiar with the immortality of the soul from Kant's discussion of the Paralogisms in the first *Critique*. Here in his moral theory, his view is that although no one can prove that the soul is immortal, the soul's immortality must be postulated to fulfill our duty. Without this postulate, one cannot expect the realm of ends to be realized.

The culminating interest in Kant's moral theory, however, resides at an even more demanding level than rendering the realm of ends into a reality. This interest is to create 'the highest good', or what Kant sometimes calls the 'kingdom of God', (i.e., the 'realm of God'). It is a perfect society where everyone's worthiness to be happy in the realm of ends is brought to fruition with everyone actually being happy in proportion to that worthiness.

How then, Kant asks, is this highest good possible? His answer is that the harmony of duty and happiness entails that we presuppose (1) the conditions necessary for a world where everyone always acts only from duty, and (2) the conditions necessary for coordinating this thoroughly moral world with happiness, which is what the members of this perfected moral world deserve.

Postulating the soul's immortality renders possible the first of these two requirements, namely, the realm of ends where everyone acts only from duty. The second is more of a challenge, since happiness is not implied by acting from duty alone. All of humanity might act with virtually a holy will and deserve to be happy, but no happiness need be forthcoming. To render possible the complete harmony of happiness and duty, or alternatively described, nature and morality, in the highest good, Kant maintains that we must postulate an all-knowing, all-good and all-powerful intelligence which can coordinate nature and morality into a single system. This is God, whose existence becomes morally necessary thereby. The starry skies above and the moral law within ultimately coincide through God.

Key idea: The highest good:

Kant envisions an idealized world where everyone acts rationally, purely from a sense of duty. Although everyone deserves to be happy in such a world, it could still be that many will remain unhappy, owing to the accidents of nature. Contrary to this imperfect situation, the highest good is a condition where everyone acts from a sense of duty and is awarded happiness in due proportion. To render the highest good possible, Kant postulates God's existence as an all-good, all-powerful, all-knowing being.

We have now come full circle. Maintaining a scepticism that denies metaphysical knowledge, the *Critique of Pure Reason* establishes that we cannot know through any logical, mathematical or scientific proofs that we are free, that the soul is immortal or that there is a God. The *Critique of Practical Reason* and Kant's other moral works give these same questions a positive answer, arguing that the consciousness of our duty entails that we postulate freedom, immortality and God. Kant is a traditional theist who believes in God's existence. His larger-scale argument across his first and second *Critiques* is that the pathway to God and the perfect society is through neither science nor the traditional metaphysical arguments for God's existence, but through moral awareness.

2 Virtue

When Kant initially speaks of the good will in the *Groundwork*, he mentions that to have a good will is not merely to have virtues such as courage and perseverance. These are morally neutral, useable by good and bad alike. After having established that the good will acts exclusively from a feeling of respect for law itself, Kant defines virtue within the context of his own theory as *the willpower to act exclusively from duty*. This is the Kantian meaning of virtue, which defines human morality at its highest stage.

Since some people have a relatively stronger capacity than others to control their inclinations and resist temptation, virtue is a matter of degree. In the preface to his later work, *The Metaphysical Principles of Virtue* (1797), Kant ascribes a 'Herculean strength' to our feeling of self-respect in its potentiality to overcome 'vice-breeding inclinations', and by implication, to virtue as the expression of that strength. Virtue is a kind of fortitude: it is the capacity to resist a strong and unjust opponent, which in this case, is our animal nature insofar as it distracts us from duty.

The third formulation of the categorical imperative states that each person is an end in itself. Each person, that is, has an intrinsic value that needs always to be respected, even though, of course, we inevitably use other people instrumentally in daily life. The 'realm' of ends is accordingly the system of mutually respecting people. Insofar as we act from duty, our aims always include respect towards other people and ourselves.

Kant accordingly has some observations that bear on realizing the highest good. Although happiness is independent of duty, virtue is nonetheless easily threatened under certain unhappy circumstances. This generates a duty to cultivate our capacities so that we are in the best worldly shape to act from duty. If we find ourselves without sufficient money, for instance, we might begin to lie and steal to survive. If we allow our health to deteriorate, then discouragement and mean-spiritedness could follow. Kant describes the duty to cultivate one's capacities as a 'duty of virtue'. It is not as steadfastly obligatory as the duties not to tell lies or to commit suicide, which are 'perfect' duties. Duties of virtue are imperfect duties that we should try to uphold as best as we can.

Another duty of virtue is to promote the happiness of others when this will sustain or enhance their virtue. The duty is also imperfect, since it does not signify that to increase the happiness of others, we should offer alcohol to an alcoholic, extra pillows to the sluggard, or weapons to the bully. The proper execution of imperfect duties is complicated, and the exercise of judgement that it requires renders the mechanically firm application of the categorical imperative less useful. We are left rather to manage our imperfect duties in view of the overall spirit of Kant's moral theory – a war between rational intellect and fleshly inclination – through wisdom and balanced judgement.

The following excerpt effectively condenses the lifestyle and personal attitudes that Kant's moral theory envisions. With respect to the excerpt's concluding sentence, which distantly echoes the Biblical episode about the worship of the golden calf, we can once again recall the first of the Ten Commandments. The contemporary philosophical difference is that in the true spirit of the Enlightenment, our reason itself is considered to be divine:

> *Do not become the slaves of other men. Do not allow your rights to be trampled underfoot by others with impunity. Make no debts that you are unable to repay. Receive no favours you can dispense with, and be neither parasites nor flatterers nor – for they differ but in degree – beggars. Live, then, frugally, lest one day you become destitute... Kneeling or prostrating oneself on the ground, even to express adoration of celestial objects, is contrary to human dignity; as is also the worshipping of them by images. For then you humble yourself, not before an ideal, the handiwork of your reason, but beneath an idol...*
> [The Metaphysical Principles of Virtue, Part One, Section 12].

3 The problem of evil

When Kant postulates God's existence as a condition for achieving the perfect harmony of duty and happiness in the highest good, he conceives of God traditionally as an all-knowing (omniscient), all-powerful (omnipotent) and all-good (omnibenevolent) being, located beyond the spatio-temporal world as its commanding source. Upon postulating such a divinity, an independent and difficult question concerning the existence of evil in the spatio-temporal world quickly presents itself: 'If there is such a God, then why is there any evil *at all*?'

This question defines the 'the problem of evil', an approach to which can be taken from either a philosophical or theological angle. The philosophical approach asks generally whether the existence of evil is compatible with God's existence, allowing that evil's very existence could constitute a *prima facie* argument against God's existence. The theological approach assumes that God exists, and asks how God and evil could be compatible under that assumption. To the extent that Kant advocates the moral argument for God's existence, he is committed to a theological approach to the problem.

The most testing aspect of the problem of evil does not concern the evil that people themselves bring into the world through their immorality, but the evil caused by natural phenomena such as disease, earthquakes, floods, droughts and tornadoes that exists independently of the human will. This is natural evil as opposed to moral evil, and it is presumably caused by God as the creator of the laws of nature. The perennially perplexing question is how an all-knowing, all-powerful, all-good being could allow such natural evil to exist. If all-knowing, then God knows how to remove the natural evil; if all-powerful, then God can remove the natural evil; if all-good, then God would presumably want to remove the natural evil.

Near the end of his career, Kant devoted an essay to the problem of evil, entitled 'On the Miscarriage of all Philosophical Trials in Theodicy' (1791). It appeared a year after the third *Critique*, the *Critique of the Power of Judgement*, in which Kant develops the related theme of how beauty and living things reinforce our belief in the compatibility between morality and mechanically driven nature.

The essay's response to the problem of evil continues to express Kant's critical philosophy, as he denies the possibility of any metaphysical solution. Following the example of the Antinomies in the Transcendental Dialectic of the *Critique of Pure Reason*, he argues that we can prove *neither* the compatibility *nor* the incompatibility of God and evil. Proofs to either conclusion require metaphysical knowledge that is beyond our rational capacities. Kant consequently rejects the metaphysical justifications to humans of God's ways – he rejects all 'theodicies' – that purport to tell us definitively about God's ultimate purposes or reasons.

We can remember that in the first *Critique*, reason's inability to obtain metaphysical knowledge redirects our attention from time-wasting metaphysical speculation, towards the more important practical application of reason in moral activity. Kant's discussion of the problem of evil follows the same pattern: after arguing that the metaphysical attempts to resolve the problem are hopeless, he turns towards morality for some wisdom. In light of the problem of evil's theoretical inscrutability, Kant defuses the problem by highlighting the implications of his moral theory.

Key idea: The three postulates of practical reason:

Kant consistently asks of his main subject matters, *How is it possible?* With respect to the question of how moral awareness is possible, he maintains (1) that we must assume that people are free as a condition for moral praise and blame, (2) that they are immortal as a condition for completely fulfilling their duty, and (3) that God exists as a condition for realizing the highest good. Freedom, immortality and God are thereby the three postulates of practical reason.

Our moral awareness makes it our duty to aim for the highest good, which requires that we postulate freedom, God and the immortality of the soul. The spatio-temporal world within which we must achieve this goal, however, contains both spiritually enlivening beauty and debilitating horror. As beauty stimulates the confidence that God and evil are compatible, the outrageous suffering in the world introduces undermining doubts. To find a way through this ambivalent situation, where earthquakes and other natural disasters sometimes occur on the most beautiful, enlivening, sunny afternoons, Kant reflects upon the Biblical story of Job.

Spotlight: The Book of Job

The Book of Job (c. sixth century BCE) is part of the Old Testament and a classic of world literature which asks, 'Why do the righteous suffer'? It touches the soul of every human being, as it portrays the plight of a good person who suffers tremendous loss at the hands of natural disasters and criminals while still retaining his faith. Insofar as everyone in the world suffers unexplainably upon occasion, and as a rule, not as intensely as did Job, the story encapsulates the human condition most disconcertingly. This enormously influential text has been the subject of commentaries from thinkers such as Pope Gregory I (540–604), Maimonides (1135–1204), Martin Luther (1483–1546), Søren Kierkegaard (1813–1855), Lev Shestov (1866–1938), and Martin Buber (1878–1965).

At the story's outset, Job is happy. He is successful, powerful, healthy, and secure. He is also righteous and believes in God. To test whether Job is truly righteous, or righteous only because he is happy, God robs Job in the worst way of everything that is materially satisfying. He loses his thousands of animals, his ten children and is infected with disease. Despite his staggering misfortune, Job does not lose his sense of dignity, which God cannot rob.

We can see why the story of Job attracted Kant. Notice how the structure of Job's experience coincides with our description of Kant's philosophical method of taking some object, and abstracting away the sensory qualities to arrive at a non-sensory core, knowable *a priori*. Kant arrived at the empty forms of space and time in this manner, as we know from the arguments in the Transcendental Aesthetic. The story of Job proceeds in the same way: we have a person, originally richly filled with sensory pleasures and worldly satisfactions, who is stripped down materially to leave nothing but a moral core that remains intact and independent of worldly satisfactions. In this stripped-down condition, utterly devoid of happiness, Kant is intrigued by Job's attitude towards God and the world's evil.

Job retains his faith in God, as he stands empty-handed materially, with nothing left but a moral consciousness marked by personal dignity and autonomy. Job remains honest, sincere, aware of the limits of his knowledge, and steadfast in his righteousness throughout his terrible trials. He makes no effort to justify why God has brought disaster upon him – and indeed, the situation to him makes no sense – but humbly accepts God's will. In the end, Job is rewarded.

Kant's moral theory does well in explaining Job's surprising intensity of faith. Indeed, one cannot help but wonder whether Kant's moral theory touches upon a profound truth, precisely because it explains Job's faith so well. If moral awareness requires generally that we postulate God's existence, then a *purified* moral awareness, stripped down of worldly happiness, would produce a correspondingly intense belief in God. No one with a consciousness of this purified moral kind will be questioning whether God exists in the face of evil, for the unconditionally grounded moral awareness that stands alone in its purity, separated from worldly happiness, produces an unshakeable faith in God. Following directly is an unshakeable faith in the compatibility of God and natural evil. Insofar as one's moral awareness is unquestionable, so is the conviction that God and evil are compatible.

Kant's interpretation of the Book of Job leaves us with the following message: the best way to come to grips with evil is to cultivate one's virtue in the face of the world's horrors. The stronger one's virtue and the more morally purified one's consciousness becomes, the greater will be one's belief in God. The resulting faith will act as a shield against debilitation and discouragement by the presence of the world's natural evil. In sum, as virtue fills one's character, the less the problem of evil presents itself as a problem.

Dig Deeper

Karl Ameriks and Otfried Hoeffe (eds.), *Kant's Moral and Legal Philosophy* (Cambridge University Press, 2009)

Andreas Føllesdal and Reidar Maliks (eds.), *Kantian Theory and Human Rights* (Routledge, 2014)

Christine Korsgaard, *Creating the Kingdom of Ends* (Cambridge University Press, 1996)

Robert Louden, *Kant's Impure Ethics: From Rational Beings to Human Beings* (Oxford University Press, 2000)

Allen Wood, *Kant's Moral Religion* (Cornell University Press, 1970)

Study questions

1 One can act, for example, 'as an individual person' or 'as a human being in general'. What is the difference between the two?

2 Why is the realm of ends not the same as the highest good?

3 Why is the kingdom of ends (the realm of ends) not structured like a monarchy?

4 What are the three postulates that our moral awareness requires?

5 What is Kant's moral argument for God's existence?

6 How does Kant define virtue?

7 Why is virtue a kind of fortitude? What kind of opponent are we resisting?

8 Why does Kant believe that we have duties to develop our talents and to help other people to be happy? Why are these duties 'imperfect'?

9 How does the Biblical story of Job relate to the problem of evil?

10 Why does Kant believe that developing our virtue is an effective way to face the problem of evil?

Section Four:

What is the meaning of beauty?

13

Beauty in its formal purity

Kant's theory of beauty is motivated by the idea that when we make a judgement of beauty, we always expect others to agree with us. This chapter will discuss how Kant's analysis of judgements of beauty accounts for this ascription of universal validity. To explain the demand that others agree, Kant restricts our attention to the object's spatio-temporal form, which everyone in all times and places can appreciate. He then locates the beauty of the object in the systematic structure of its spatio-temporal form, maintaining that when the object is judged aesthetically and disinterestedly, simply in terms of how its systematic form makes us feel, we experience a pleasurable harmony between our faculties of understanding and imagination. This harmony is a cognitive feeling that one can expect everyone to experience.

Dramatic sunsets, sexually alluring faces, well-toned bodies, idyllic landscapes, star-filled skies, flowers, and perhaps cuddly babies, puppies and kittens may come to mind when we think of beauty. If we were to teach the word 'beautiful' to a youngster, we might show the child a rose or a spiral seashell, or point to a setting sun on a painted horizon, or to a softly lit, full moon rising in the opposite distance soon thereafter.

Beauty remains difficult to comprehend nonetheless. In any theory of beauty, we expect to learn why we call these items, along with many others, 'beautiful'. Kant's peculiarity is that although he is rightly celebrated as the father of modern aesthetics, his driving philosophical interests are not fundamentally in aesthetic theory, which came to him later in life. His career is defined rather by the broader systematic concerns that surround the relationship between science and morality. Kant's theory of human knowledge as well as his ethics – his perpetual awe of the starry skies above and the moral law within – underpin and inform the theories of beauty and fine art for which the third *Critique*, the *Critique of the Power of Judgement* (1790), is well known.

A good part of Kant's philosophy of beauty is thus geared to explain how our experiences of beauty, both natural and artistic, reinforce our scientific and moral endeavours. An unexpected consequence is that only a handful of the features we ordinarily regard as constitutive of beauty become characteristic of what we may refer to within Kant's aesthetics as 'pure beauty'. The features that we ordinarily recognize as constitutive of beauty which he does not include, such as a rose's pastel colours, soft textures and delicate perfume, have a place in his theory, but they are secondary to the rarefied conception of pure beauty upon which he grounds his aesthetics.

To appreciate Kant's account of pure beauty, it helps again to revisit the abstractive philosophical method he employs to reveal space and time as forms within the human mind. In the *Critique of Pure Reason*, the section on the transcendental aesthetic begins with the consideration of any ordinary object, and proceeds to isolate the object's fundamental constituents for separate philosophical treatment. In his philosophical analysis,

Kant considers the object's sensory qualities (e.g., its colours, odours, textures, tastes) apart from its geometrical shape or formal design, and sets the sensory qualities and the spatio-temporal design apart from the meaning-lending concepts that we project onto the object. These three layers – (1) the object's sensory qualities, (2) its spatio-temporal structure and (3) its conceptual meanings – emerge from Kant's analysis as separate subjects for philosophical treatment.

Upon this threefold layering of sensation, form and meaning, Kant constructs his theory of beauty. He first highlights the object's spatio-temporal design as the locus of pure beauty, and then, moving on to consider more complex varieties of beauty, he reintroduces the object's sensory and semantic dimensions insofar as they blend in with pure beauty. We will keep this procedure in mind.

At a more cursory level, Kant's theory of beauty is inspired by an ordinary, but crucial, observation about our daily aesthetic practice: when, of some object, we assert that it is beautiful, we typically think that others ought to agree. Kant regards this as virtually a demand that we make of others, and he is captivated by the persistent strength of this demand, which is almost moral in tone.

The situation is unlike our personal reports about whether we enjoy the taste of, for instance, chocolate, licorice, mashed potatoes, spicy foods, frog's legs, lamb's brains, caviar, wines, or thick soups. In such cases, we do not automatically press upon others to agree, and the reason is obvious: other people's tongues, eyes, fingertips, ears and noses can be more sensitively or alternatively conditioned than our own, and vice-versa. If someone's eyes cannot physiologically register certain shades of colour, no one can reasonably maintain that the person ought to be sensitive to those shades in their aesthetic judgements. Applying here as well, is the dictum that 'ought' implies 'can', for if one cannot, then certainly one ought not.

In view of people's physiological differences, that we normally expect others to agree with our judgements of beauty signals to Kant that these judgements are grounded differently from reports of sensory likings or dislikings. He can only infer that, like moral judgements, they involve feelings that originate in a different part of the mind, independently of the particular construction of our sensory organs. The upshot is to divide aesthetic judgements into two elementary groups, that of 'aesthetic judgements of *beauty*' and 'aesthetic judgements of *sensation*', where the latter refer to our private sensory likings. As 'aesthetic', both aesthetic judgements of beauty and aesthetic judgements of sensation are based on feelings, but Kant is convinced that radically different kinds of feelings are respectively involved.

With this distinction in hand, Kant can more effectively explain why the particular quality of the feelings associated with beauty generates the expectation that others agree with our judgements. One could say that the feeling of beauty is a *feeling of universal validity* that constitutes our experience of a beautiful object. When we assert that some object is beautiful, the feeling of conviction is strong, closely akin to that felt in asserting $2 + 2 = 4$, or that parallel lines on a flat surface never meet. In contrast, ordinary sensory feelings lack this socially univocal and demanding dimension, since people's sense organs are variously constructed. Sensory feelings are particular to each of us as individuals, and they harbour no expectations that others ought to feel the same way.

Key idea: 'Aesthetic judgements of sense' as opposed to 'aesthetic judgements of beauty':

Although all aesthetic judgements are based on feelings, Kant identifies two different kinds of feelings which can be the ground of such judgements. These are sensory feelings, which vary from person to person, and the feeling of pure beauty – a special cognitive feeling which does not vary from person to person.

Let us then explore this feeling of universal validity that characterizes judgements of beauty. There are three aspects to take into account. First, we will need some further details about the internal sources of this universal feeling that supposedly can be exactly the same in everyone. Second, with respect to the external objects that we judge, we will need to restrict our attention to features of objects that are equally accessible to all human beings *per se*, independently of the physiological variations in people's sense organs. Third, in our approach to the objects, we will need to adopt an appropriately universalistic attitude when judging those objects in reference to their beauty – an attitude that promotes a universal feeling by disregarding all personal or idiosyncratic factors. Within Kant's theory of beauty, these three aspects work together.

We can start with the third, which concerns the appropriate attitude – an 'aesthetic' attitude, one may call it – required to allow an object's pure beauty to impress itself upon us clearly. Here, perhaps surprisingly to some, Kant states that when we judge an object's pure beauty, it is not necessary to know what kind of thing the object is! The object's formal design can in itself be satisfying to apprehend, independently of any such information. Knowing that the object happens to be an amethyst or a piece of rose quartz, for example, does not affect how we feel about the object's spatio-temporal configuration, when the object's configuration is considered in isolation.

Neither, curiously, do we need to know that the object is real, since a mental image that is structurally identical to a real object would be equally as satisfying to behold, if we are restricting our attention to the sheer quality of the design. In this respect, judgements of beauty presuppose a 'disinterested' attitude, where one remains neutral about whether or not the object actually exists. Dreams can be as beautiful as the real world.

Spotlight: Aesthetic disinterestedness and the aesthetic attitude

In asserting that judgements of beauty should be made 'without interest', Kant asks us to suspend our interest in the object's being real. This is a small departure from previous theorists who also associated disinterestedness with a properly aesthetic attitude, most of whom were British and writing during the late 1600s and early 1700s. Among these aesthetic attitude theorists are Anthony

Ashley-Cooper (1621–1683), who was the first Earl of Shaftesbury, Joseph Addison (1672–1719) and Francis Hutcheson (1694–1746).

In their discussions of beauty, 'disinterestedness' refers to a selfless attitude that leaves one free to appreciate objects and activities for their own sake, without any view towards possessing the objects or using them for material gain.

Ever since the 1600s, this idea of an aesthetic attitude wherein one divests oneself of selfish motives and appreciates objects for their own sake has been central to aesthetic theory. Along with Kant, Shaftesbury is frequently mentioned as the father of modern aesthetics – we might refer to Shaftesbury as the grandfather – precisely owing to his insights about aesthetic disinterestedness.

Finally – and this runs contrary to our ordinary conception of beauty – if we are to judge an object aesthetically in a universalistic manner, then we need to disregard the object's colours and other sensory qualities. Otherwise, colour-blind people, for example, will not in principle be able to agree with our judgements, contrary to the feeling of universal validity associated with beauty that extends to all people.

That Kant, by and large, excludes colours from pure beauty is a surprising dimension of his aesthetic theory. He regards colours merely as 'charms' that can either assist or interfere with our disinterested contemplation of an object's spatio-temporal design, but in either case, do not constitute the object's pure beauty. Thinking in terms of what we must presuppose to account for our feeling of universal validity, Kant restricts an object's pure beauty to its spatio-temporal form, cognizant of how the forms of space and time, along with the geometrical and mathematical propositions that issue from them, are identically structured in all human beings.

For example, if an ancient Egyptian were to reflect exclusively upon the spatio-temporal design of some crystal, and if some person from a later century, having been raised in a different culture and speaking a different language, were to reflect upon the same crystal in a museum, we could nonetheless reasonably expect the two to agree in their aesthetic judgements. By setting aside colours (i.e., sensory qualities), concepts and culture, the way is cleared for everyone to agree.

Having described the appropriate aesthetic attitude for making judgements of pure beauty – an attitude focused exclusively and disinterestedly upon an object's spatio-temporal form – we can now consider Kant's explanation of the feeling of universal validity that underlies our experience of beauty. As we can recall from his theory of knowledge, the categories of the understanding inform our experience with a deterministic structure when they are projected upon given sensory inputs. These pure concepts, or categories, introduce universal validity into our experience. Concretely, these concepts do so after being infused with a temporal form – after they are 'schematized' or 'aestheticized' – that renders them compatible with sensory inputs given by the imagination in conjunction with our sensibility.

Kant analyses this situation by saying that for any judgement that yields detailed knowledge of the world, two faculties of mind must coordinate with each other, hand-in-hand. The first is the faculty that supplies concepts, the understanding. The second is the imagination, the faculty that, construed in conjunction with the faculty of sensibility, presents constructed sensory images, or 'intuitions', to the understanding for the purposes of comprehension. To have empirical knowledge, then, understanding and imagination must operate in conjunction with one another, not unlike how a sheet of rolled out cookie dough (analogous to the sensory inputs) must operate compatibly, or 'in harmony', with the action of a cookie-cutter (analogous to the comprehending concepts of the understanding) for the purpose of making cookies (analogous to the resulting empirical judgements).

When the faculties of understanding and imagination are working in solid harmony, a general feeling of satisfaction issues from our being in a favourable position to know the world. This is a 'cognitive' rather than sensory feeling, and as knowing human beings, Kant believes that everyone experiences it in the same way. This parallels the moral context, where similarly, everyone experiences the feeling of respect for themselves.

Hence follows the demand that others ought to agree with our judgements of beauty. The key to Kant's theory of beauty resides here, in the *a priori* feeling generated by the harmony of the cognitive faculties of the understanding and imagination – the faculties that operate in conjunction to generate empirical judgements about the world such as 'the leaf is green' or 'the sky is blue'.

Key idea: The harmony of the cognitive faculties:

The special cognitive feeling associated with judgements of beauty issues from a 'free play' or harmonious general accord between the two faculties which operate when we apply concepts to intuitions in an act of judgement. These are the faculties of understanding and imagination.

Kant further maintains that in reference exclusively to their spatio-temporal design, certain objects present an appearance that we recognize as being especially compatible with our desire to know the world. Indeed, these objects' structures appear to be naturally fitted to our cognitive faculties, almost as if some higher intelligence had this purpose in mind for the objects. In view of their satisfying structure, these objects cause the understanding and imagination to resonate together harmoniously, setting them in an optimal condition and position to know the world.

As we can now infer, this resonance of the understanding and imagination is the feeling of universal validity that Kant identifies with the experience of pure beauty. The feeling of pure beauty is a feeling of universal validity that issues from the harmony of the cognitive faculties of the understanding and imagination, caused by our apprehension of an object that appears to be especially fitted to those faculties. In essence, pure beauty arouses and encourages our cognition.

Our next question is: What kinds of objects cause this cognitive resonance and beautiful feeling? To answer this, we can remember how our faculty of reason aims to systematize all of our knowledge. The broader purpose of cognition is accordingly to formulate a complete system of scientific knowledge which can predict every event. This is an ideal towards which we cognitively aim, and it is crucial to Kant's theory of beauty.

Although the categories of the understanding stabilize our experience in a deterministic way, it remains uncertain that a single, seamlessly integrated system will emerge from the laws of nature that we formulate. We surely aim to construct such a system, but there is always the worry that nature might not agree with our cognitive intentions. Kant sometimes expresses amazement that our experience is not more chaotic than it is, despite how the categories of the understanding organize the sensory manifold. Our mind's structure may compel us to regard nature as being thoroughly deterministic, but it is another matter to specify the determinism's exact mechanism in the presence of so many contingent details.

As a cognitive principle, then, Kant holds that we must assume that nature is thoroughly systematizable for the sake of advancing and completing our scientific knowledge. For a perfect science, we must assume that rationality permeates experience. This leads Kant to recognize as the ultimate source of that permeating rationality, a supreme intelligence as nature's author and governor. To guide scientific thought towards its completely systematic end, we must suppose that everything in nature has a purpose, that these purposes integrate into a single system, and that the system itself is the expression of a divine understanding.

Kant refers to this science-enabling assumption as the 'principle of the purposiveness of nature'. Our cognitive faculties of the understanding and imagination can operate maximally, only if nature is thoroughly fitted to our scientific quest for total comprehension. Assuming that nature *is* so fitted is none other than to regard nature as a work of divine art. Just as we need to assume that God exists for the sake of making happiness possible for everyone who acts morally, we need to assume that God exists for the sake of constructing a seamlessly predictable, comprehensive system of natural laws.

Not all objects are well-organized in their structure, so as to appear especially fitted to our cognitive faculties. Some are disorganized and frustrating to comprehend. However, the well-organized objects – we can think of snowflakes, flowers, crystals and abstract designs of all sorts – in their fortuitous display of systematic form, stand as reinforcements and confirmations that nature is amenable to our quest for systematic knowledge. Pure beauty thereby inspires science. The systematicity of these objects' forms resonates with our cognitive faculties to set them into harmony with one another and to generate the feeling of pure beauty.

Such systematically organized objects look as if they were designed. As such, they have a 'purposive' form and appear to be works of art. As noted, to judge their pure beauty, we need not know what kinds of thing they are, and accordingly, what purposes they serve, if any. Purely beautiful objects display a purposiveness (i.e., a 'designedness') without our having to specify any particular purpose for the objects. They display a 'purposiveness without purpose', as Kant states. When apprehended as such, their designs resonate freely with our cognitive faculties, setting them into harmony with one another to produce a feeling of universal validity. Encountering a purely beautiful object in nature is thus like looking into a mirror, for the beautiful object's systematic structure appears as a kindred spirit that to our satisfaction, reflects our rational selves. In beauty, we see a reflection of our humanity.

Kant defines the faculty of judgement – the main subject of the third *Critique* – as the faculty of subsuming individuals under concepts. We employ this faculty when we observe diverse phenomena and comprehend them under a single law of nature. When through further reflection, we integrate individual laws of nature into a scientific system under a single universal principle, we employ our judgement as well.

When we apprehend a systematic design, and feel our cognitive faculties resonating in view of the design in the feeling of beauty, we experience in an abstract, indeterminate form, the universally valid process of finding a concept for some given individual. Kant refers to this resonance as the 'free play' of the imagination and understanding. Rather than comprehending the object's design as the expression of some determinate purpose, the feeling of universal validity is subsumed under the general thought that nature is fitted for our comprehension. In our judgements of pure beauty, the feeling of beauty is subsumed under the principle of the purposiveness of nature.

Key idea: Purposiveness without purpose:

An object which effectively stimulates the harmony of the cognitive faculties has a systematic form, which makes it look like it was intentionally designed. The object accordingly displays a 'purposiveness' in its design, although no actual purpose need be present for us to appreciate how it appears to be the product of some intelligence. This display of a 'purposiveness without purpose' in an object's design is the source of the object's pure beauty.

We have been speaking up until this point about the dynamics of *pure* beauty. This rarefied notion of beauty is defined exclusively in reference to an object's spatio-temporal form, independently of the object's sensory qualities and meanings. Upon this foundation, Kant extends his aesthetic theory by considering more complicated varieties of beauty which involve not only the object's spatio-temporal form, but sensory qualities and meanings in conjunction with that form. It is to these various kinds of beauty that we will now turn.

Dig Deeper

Henry Allison, *Kant's Theory of Taste: A Reading of the Critique of Aesthetic Judgement* (Cambridge University Press, 2001)

Paul Crowther, *The Kantian Aesthetic: From Knowledge to the Avant-Garde* (Oxford University Press, 2010)

Paul Guyer, *Kant and the Claims of Taste* (Harvard University Press, 1979)

Eva Shaper, *Studies in Kant's Aesthetics* (Edinburgh University Press, 1979)

John Zammito, *The Genesis of Kant's Critique of Judgement* (University of Chicago Press, 1992)

Study questions

1. What is the difference between 'aesthetic judgements of beauty' and 'aesthetic judgements of sensation'?

2. Why does Kant believe that the feeling of beauty is a feeling of universal validity?

3. Why does Kant say that we need to judge the beauty of things 'disinterestedly'?

4. When judging an object's pure beauty, why is it not necessary to know what kind of object it is?

5. What is the relationship between the feeling of universal validity and the harmony of the cognitive faculties?

6. What is the principle of the purposiveness of nature, and why is it important for scientific inquiry?

7. Why does science require us to regard nature as a work of art?

8. Why do all purely beautiful objects exhibit a 'purposiveness without purpose'?

9. What is the significance of the 'free play' of the imagination and understanding in Kant's theory of pure beauty?

10. Are human beauty and the beauty of fine art examples of pure beauty?

14

Human beauty and fine art

Kant's account of pure beauty refers us to an object's spatio-temporal design, considered independently of the object's variable sensory qualities, and independently of the kind of object it happens to be. In many cases, however, we make judgements of beauty with these sensory and conceptual factors in mind. The beauty of colourful roses and sunsets, human beauty and fine art would be examples. This chapter will describe how Kant elaborates upon his canonical account of pure beauty to include the more complicating sensory and conceptual aspects of beautiful objects. Fine art, which Kant describes as the product of artistic geniuses who produce 'aesthetic ideas', is central to his discussion.

1 Beauty mixed with sensory and conceptual content

Kant's theory of pure beauty describes the conditions under which any human being can judge an object's beauty and legitimately expect all other humans to agree. Cultural, linguistic, psychological and physiological differences are set aside, and exclusive attention is paid to the object's spatio-temporal form. Although strictly circumscribed, the resulting aesthetic is universalistic in its formalism, and it captures some of the familiar examples to which we apply the word 'beauty'. The theory explains well why we regard snowflakes, seashells, crystals and all sorts of abstract designs as beautiful, owing to their rationally organized structure. The beauty of roses and sunsets, however, remains in need of further explanation, as does human beauty. The beauty of fine art, when judged as art, also requires a more elaborate account.

Kant, obviously, does not believe that the beauty of roses, sunsets, human beauty and fine art can be fully understood in sole reference to pure beauty. To fill out his theory and to account for such examples, he formulates two kinds of 'mixed' or 'combinatory' forms of beauty that widen his basic notion of pure beauty. The procedure is straightforward: calling upon his threefold division of spatio-temporal form, sensation and meaning, and using his conception of pure beauty as the ground, he considers the contemplation of an object's spatio-temporal design in conjunction with (1) reflections on the object's sensory qualities and (2) reflections on the object's kind. The first combination gives us a conception of beauty that applies to objects such as roses and sunsets. The second yields a conception that covers human beauty and fine art.

The mixture of spatio-temporal form and sensory qualities in the first combination provides an account of the beauty of things such as roses and sunsets, since the rose's delicate texture, perfume and colour, for example, now enter into consideration with its design. Kant is reluctant to refer to this fusion as beautiful in a genuine sense, since the term 'beauty' implies that we can legitimately expect others to agree with our judgements.

Once we introduce sensory qualities into our judgement of an object's beauty – qualities that vary unpredictably from person to person – we lose the legitimacy of that universalistic expectation. For lack of a label for this kind of beauty, we can refer to it as 'unrefined' beauty, since the object's sensory qualities are intermingled with the appreciation of the object's structural qualities. When judging aesthetically such admixtures of structural and sensory qualities, one cannot reasonably expect others to agree with one's judgements of beauty.

In this aesthetic mixture of sensation with design, the colours (for example) can play different roles. They can remain in the background and function mainly to enhance our perception of an object's delineation, supporting our judgement of pure beauty, or, at the other end of the continuum, they can permeate the object's appearance to obscure our perception of the object's spatio-temporal form. The beauty of sunsets is a revealing case of the latter. Given how a sunset's colours typically predominate within its appearance, this kind of 'beauty' turns out to be the lowest kind in Kant's theory. In Kant's precise language, we should refer to the pleasing sensory qualities of sunsets as 'charming' or 'agreeable', rather than as beautiful.

Sunsets are nonetheless among our paradigm cases of beauty, and this suggests either that Kant is wrongheaded to locate sunsets at the lower levels of beauty, or that he correctly reveals that our delight over such things as beautiful sunsets, sparkling fireworks, and the multicoloured lights that decorate houses, windows and trees during the holiday season, betrays an unrefined sense of taste.

In the same way, music does not fare well within Kant's aesthetics. Thinking of how people are often pleased – one should say 'charmed' – by the sheer sound of musical instruments, as when appreciating a mellow French horn, a spooky oboe, a dreamy sitar, or a sensitive violin, he describes music as an art which 'occupies the lowest place among the fine arts (just as it occupies perhaps the highest place among those that are judged according to their agreeableness), because it merely plays with sensations' (*Critique of Judgement*, Section 53).

Spotlight: Aesthetic formalism

Kant is frequently referred to as a 'formalist' in aesthetic theory, and correctly so, as he defines pure beauty – a quality that natural objects, dream images and works of art can equally possess – in reference to an object's spatio-temporal form. In more recent aesthetic theory, the term 'formalism' is typically used not in reference to defining *beauty*, however, but more narrowly in defining *art*. A classic example is found in the writings of the British art critic, Clive Bell (1881–1964), who wrote the following:

> *What quality is shared by all objects that provoke our aesthetic emotions? What quality is common to Sta. Sophia and the windows at Chartres, Mexican sculpture, a Persian bowl, Chinese carpets, Giotto's frescoes at Padua, and the masterpieces of Poussin, Piero della Francesca, and Cézanne? Only one answer seems possible – significant form. In each, lines and colours combined in a particular way, certain forms and relations of forms, stir our aesthetic emotions. These relations and combinations of lines and colours, these aesthetically moving forms, I call 'Significant Form'; and 'Significant Form' is the one quality common to all works of visual art. (Clive Bell, Art (1914), Chapter I, 'The Aesthetic Hypothesis')*

Notice how Bell includes colours within the realm of 'form', as do most contemporary formalists, whereas Kant sets colours aside as merely sensory charms, restricting his attention to the object's spatial and temporal configuration. When discussing Kant's formalism is it important to keep distinct these two projects of defining *beauty* as opposed to defining *art*.

Kant's interest in mixed modes of beauty is less concerned with music and sunsets, than with the second kind of combination mentioned above, namely, those cases where a conceptual factor enters into our judgement of beauty. Here, we judge an object's beauty in view of the kind of thing it is. Suppose someone draws our aesthetic attention to a snowflake which has a few broken points. We can judge the snowflake's beauty in reference to its pure design, or we can judge its beauty 'as' a snowflake, including in the latter judgement, a comparison of the given snowflake's design with an idealized image of what snowflakes are supposed to look like.

In the first case, we make a judgement of pure beauty. If the snowflake's design happens to be well-balanced, systematically organized, complicated, etc., then the broken points, as 'broken', will not disturb the aesthetic quality, since our judgement attends only to the object's bare configuration. In the second case, we make a judgement that adheres to the kind of thing we are judging, and since ideal snowflakes have no broken points, the broken points on our given snowflake will detract from its beauty. The very same design can thus be judged as beautiful, or as not very beautiful, depending upon whether we judge it purely or in relation to the kind of thing it is.

In such instances of 'adherent' or 'dependent' beauty, we appreciate the object's design as in a judgement of pure beauty, except that we factor into the judgement, a comparison of the object's abstract design with an idealized image of the 'perfect specimen' of the kind of thing in question. The number of possible snowflake designs that are consistent with the ideal image of the 'perfect snowflake' is limitless, but a positive judgement of adherent beauty requires that any given snowflake's particular design does not conflict with the image of the perfect snowflake.

In the best examples of adherent beauty, a design that is purely beautiful on its own, helps make the image of the perfect specimen shine through. Such a harmonious relationship between the abstract design and the image of the perfect specimen is possible in the case of snowflakes, because the image of a perfect snowflake is itself beautifully structured. This is not true for all species of thing.

Kant's notion of adherent beauty thereby opens up some new areas for reflection and clarification. The structures of the ideal versions of naturally occurring objects are not all systematically organized and beautiful, and this introduces some further confusion in the use of the term 'beauty'. Some people would be disposed, for instance, to refer to a perfect specimen of a flea – the appearance of which is particularly unattractive, if not scary – as a 'beautiful flea', but Kant would resist this way of speaking. His theory distinguishes between beauty and perfection, just as it distinguishes between beauty and sensory charm. The sheer, but exact, match between an object's (say, a flea) structure and its ideal form, without any consideration of what the ideal form happens to look like, relates to the object's perfection, not to its beauty.

Key idea: 'Judgements of adherent beauty' versus 'judgements of free beauty':

There are at least two ways to judge an object's beauty. The first is to consider how an object's design makes us feel in view of what kind of object it is. This is a judgement of adherent beauty. The second is more simply to consider how the object's design makes us feel, without being concerned about the kind of object it is. This is a judgement of free beauty. In the first case, we adhere to and respect the object's kind. In the second, our judgement is free from considerations of the object's kind.

Let us now move to fine art, since judgements of beauty in fine art also fall under Kant's conception of adherent beauty. This is because any judgement of an artwork's beauty as *art*, rather than as a pure design, immediately introduces the concept of 'art' in connection with the object's beauty. Since 'art' signifies intentional and intelligent production, the judgement of an artwork's beauty must adhere to a concept of what the artwork's meaning is supposed to be. As such, judgements of the beauty of fine art are adherent, and are never pure.

The usual way to postulate a meaning for an artwork is in reference to the artist's intentions. Since these intentions are often unclear, the legitimacy of pressing upon other people to agree with our judgements is considerably weakened, since others' conceptions of what the artwork is supposed to mean can easily differ from our own.

In most cases, judging the beauty of an artwork does not compare well to judging the beauty of snowflakes and fleas, since we tend to have relatively clear ideas of how natural objects are supposed to look, whether they happen to be fleas, snowflakes, turtles or tulips. In fine art, the artist's intentions are less easy to determine, and so it can be difficult to decide how the work is ideally supposed to appear.

Realizing this, Kant observes that judgements of the beauty of fine art can be more universalistic if they embody humanly shared themes such as love, death, courage, friendship and suffering. By incorporating such themes into the artwork, the concepts upon which the artwork depends can be more clearly discernable and shareable by everyone. This allows the demand for universal validity that follows with the mere use of the term 'beauty', to hold more reasonably.

At this point, we have seen how Kant's conception of adherent beauty applies to the aesthetic judgement of natural objects and fine art. Human beauty is yet another example. This species of adherent beauty, moreover, is among the most direct expressions within Kant's aesthetics of the fusion of beauty and morality.

Kant maintains, as we know, that human beings are essentially rational and hence, essentially moral, since morality is a matter of rationality's practical application. This signifies for Kant that insofar as humans unconditionally ought to respect themselves, human beauty unconditionally ought to respect morality. If someone decorates his or her body with designs that obscure or conflict with natural moral expression, then despite how well the designs may be systematically organized and beautiful on their own accord, Kant maintains that their proper place is not upon a human body. His example is elaborate and extensive facial tattoos – he refers to the Maori warriors of New Zealand – that make it difficult to discern what a person's facial expression happens to be.

At first, this prescription for human beauty may sound too morally conservative to be plausible. Kant has a solid reason in its support, though, alluded to above. He identifies an unconditional dimension of our being – our rationality – that is immune to physical change and is at the basis of morality. The concept to which human beauty must adhere is therefore timelessly fixed. Insofar as we have an unconditional moral duty to respect everyone, including ourselves, Kant believes that one cannot present oneself as a humanly beautiful person, if one's appearance is marred by designs that display a lack of self-respect.

This leads to a classically inspired ideal of human beauty, central to which is the image of a physically well-proportioned and well-functioning person with a morally developed character. Here, Kant echoes the ancients in his own prescription that a beautiful human being must be both physically and morally sound. Whereas the classical expression – credited to the ancient Greek philosopher Thales (624–546 BCE) and appearing in the work of the Roman poet, Juvenal (first century CE) – reads '*mens sana in corpore sano*' ('a healthy mind in a healthy body'), Kant modifies the notion of a 'healthy mind' into that of a 'morally well-constituted mind'. This aligns his ideal of human beauty with the greater systematic project of establishing a compatibility and harmony between morality (the mind) and nature (the body), which is Kant's primary concern.

2 Artistic genius as the expression of aesthetic ideas

Although Kant acknowledges skill-centred technical arts – we can think of basket weaving, furniture making and pottery – his theory of artistic beauty leans towards fine arts such as painting, sculpture and literature. These are typically rich in meaning and serve accordingly as powerful stimulants to our imagination. Since his theory of pure beauty rests upon a non-sensory cognitive feeling that arises when the faculties of understanding and imagination are set into harmonious 'free play' with one another, Kant is motivated to account for the beauty of fine art in reference not only to its spatio-temporal form, but also in reference to how its richness of meaning stimulates our imagination. In a departure from his canonical and formalistic theory of pure beauty, he believes that the beauty of fine art involves both form and content.

One of the motivations for Kant's theory of fine art derives from an observation about the quality of the artistic images. He asserts that in high-quality fine art, the images are so multidimensional in meaning, that is it impossible adequately to capture their significance by precisely spelling it out. Expressive portraits of the quality that Rembrandt typically painted, simply defy words. Insofar as the artwork's meaning-laden images are interpretively inexhaustible, Kant maintains that they set the imagination and understanding into a free play that generates the cognitive feeling of beauty.

Kant's technical term for these richly meaningful images requires some caution in our understanding of it. He refers to the images as 'aesthetic ideas', recalling his philosophical use of the term 'idea' in the context of 'ideas of reason' – conceptual constructions that extend imaginatively and comprehensively beyond the contours of possible human experience. Our examples in earlier chapters were the rational ideas of 'soul' and 'world'. In the present usage, the meaning of 'idea' is more tempered, referring more simply to how rich aesthetic images can stimulate thoughts that are too complicated to articulate in any conclusive way:

> ...by an aesthetic idea I understand that representation of the imagination which occasions much thought, without, however, any definite thought, i.e. any concept, being capable of being adequate to it. It consequently cannot be completely compassed and made intelligible by language – we easily see that it is the counterpart (pendant) of a rational idea, which conversely is a concept to which no intuition (or representation of the imagination) can be adequate.
>
> (Critique of Judgement, Section 49)

One of the commendable aspects of Kant's analysis of fine art is his reluctance to force it too squarely into his canonical theory of pure beauty. He realizes that fine art is permeated with metaphorical expression and allusive symbolism, and that it is impossible to overlook its meanings in any plausible theory of its beauty. To account for artistic beauty, he consequently develops a conception of aesthetic ideas.

In his open-minded attention to the constitution of fine art, Kant soon finds himself in danger of losing the universality of judgements of beauty that ideally attaches to our very use of the term 'beauty'. The difficulty arises because the linguistic and cultural content of aesthetic ideas interferes with the universality of the judgements.

Recalling our earlier example, suppose that an ancient Egyptian, attending exclusively to the spatio-temporal structure of a crystal formation, judges the structure to be beautiful. Someone from a later century, disinterestedly viewing the same crystal and exclusively the same design, might easily agree. When restricting our attention to spatio-temporal structures, universal agreement is possible. In contrast, the same Egyptian, upon being presented with a fine Medieval painting of a crucifixion (if such time travel were possible), would be in no position to judge the painting's beauty as a crucifixion. If the Egyptian's faculties of imagination and understanding were to resonate to any significant extent in view of the painting, they would not be resonating for the same reasons as those of someone who appreciates the painting in light of its Christian meaning. Their respective judgements of the painting's beauty would consequently be unable to cohere with one another.

Unlike the forms of space and time with which people are naturally equipped, religious imagery is not innate, so the historically derived contents of aesthetic ideas do not support the universality of judgements of artistic beauty. Since Kant's theory of the beauty of fine art as the expression of aesthetic ideas includes this kind of historically contingent imagery, it is not conducive to judgements of beauty where we can expect all other humans to agree.

Key idea: Maintaining the universality of judgements of beauty:

Kant's theory of pure beauty restricts our attention to an object's spatio-temporal form and thereby gives us clear grounds to expect other people to agree with our judgements of beauty. In his theory of fine art, Kant tries to preserve the universality of judgements of beauty by advocating universally-recognizable subject matters, such as love, death, courage, etc. When the concepts expressed in fine art become culturally specific, however, the universality of judgements of beauty becomes more difficult to sustain.

What Kant loses in the universality of judgements of the beauty of fine art, he gains in the plausibility of his account of fine art. His description of fine art as laden with metaphorical content and as surpassing all efforts to circumscribe exact meanings, is not only convincing on the face of things. It fits well with the more modern idea that works of fine art are, in their meaningful constitution, closely comparable to dreams. Like fine art, dreams are also densely symbolic, as if a set of meanings were put into a compressor to generate a thought-provoking, significance-radiating image. As are works of fine art, dreams are endlessly interpretable.

Reinforcing the plausibility of Kant's theory of fine art is his account of artistic genius. According to Kant, artistic geniuses – people who have a special ability to generate aesthetic ideas – have a naturally powerful creative capacity, almost as if nature itself were working through these individuals to express its own intentions in works of fine art. As mentioned in connection with the principle of the purposiveness of nature, our cognitive, scientific purposes direct us to regard nature as a supreme work of art, as if it were the product of a divine intelligence. When we appreciate fine art itself, conversely, we often take pleasure in how it looks so naturally done, as opposed to appearing contrived and artificial. In this respect, the artistic genius is like the divine intelligence, albeit on a finite human scale, insofar as the genius creates a 'second nature' in the work of fine art, whose appearance looks natural.

The spontaneous and imaginative aspect of artistic creation that Kant's theory highlights, is consistent with the hypothesis that artistic creativity issues fundamentally from the unconscious part of the mind. Creative processes are typically inscrutable to the artists themselves, who often cannot explain how they arrive at their artistic insights and unique styles of expression. In dreams as well, the metaphorical content derives inexplicably from the unconscious, often as the expression of hidden desires.

Near the end of Kant's life, the concept of the 'unconscious' assumed a strong presence in the writings of other philosophers, partially due to Kant's own trailblazing in his theory of fine art. A good example is F. W. J. Schelling (1775–1854), who was familiar with Kant's third *Critique*, and who associated the artistic genius with the unconscious in his *System of Transcendental Idealism* (1800).

At the end of the nineteenth century and beginning of the twentieth, Sigmund Freud (1856–1939) explicitly developed links between the unconscious, dreams and artistic creativity in his psychoanalytic writings. Following Freud's insights about the instinctual nature of artistic creativity, the early twentieth-century surrealist movement was convinced that artistic creativity issues from the free flow of thoughts from the unconscious. Kant's theory of fine art may find it difficult to establish and maintain the universality of judgements of beauty, but in its account of fine art's profundity, it is among the most historically influential aspects of his aesthetic theory.

Dig Deeper

Ted Cohen and Paul Guyer, (eds.), *Essays in Kant's Aesthetics* (University of Chicago Press, 1982)

Paul Guyer, *Kant and the Experience of Freedom: Essays on Aesthetics and Morality* (Cambridge University Press, 1993)

Salim Kemal, *Kant and Fine Art: An Essay on Kant and the Philosophy of Fine Art and Culture* (Clarendon Press, 1986)

Rebecca Kukla (ed.), *Aesthetics and Cognition in Kant's Critical Philosophy* (Cambridge University Press, 2006)

Kenneth Rogerson, *The Problem of Free Harmony in Kant's Aesthetics* (SUNY Press, 2009)

Study questions

1 Why would Kant find it objectionable to say of a particularly brilliant and colourfully spectacular sunset, that it is 'beautiful'?

2 Is it ever proper practice to judge the beauty of a human being through a judgement of pure beauty, regarding the person simply as an abstract design?

3 Why would Kant find it objectionable for someone, upon encountering a flea that matches exactly the image of a 'perfect specimen' of a flea, to refer to it as a 'beautiful' flea?

4 What is Kant's objection to extensive facial tattoos? Is this an aesthetic or moral objection?

5 Why are all judgements of artistic beauty, judgements of adherent beauty?

6 What should an ideally beautiful human being look like, according to Kant?

7 Why does Kant locate music at the lowest level of the fine arts?

8 In Kant's view, what is an aesthetic idea?

9 Why does Kant's theory of aesthetic ideas make it difficult to make judgements of the beauty of fine art with which all human beings can be expected to agree?

10 What is the connection between 'the unconscious' and Kant's theory of artistic genius?

15

Sublimity, beauty, biology and morality

As expressed across his three *Critiques*, Kant's philosophy can be read as an extended analysis of whether a perfectly moral society can be realized. In the *Critique of Pure Reason*, he restricts the scope of scientific knowledge to the sensory world of space and time, establishing our freedom in a supersensible world beyond. In the *Critique of Practical Reason* and other moral writings, he describes our moral awareness and duties as grounded in reason, postulating God as the guarantor of worldly happiness. In the *Critique of the Power of Judgement*, he explains how the reinforcing experiences of beauty, sublimity and living organisms help compatibly to draw nature and morality together. In this chapter, we will consider these several ways in which Kant associates nature and morality in the third *Critique*.

1 Aesthetic ideas and morality

Kant formulates his theory of aesthetic ideas in view of the rich meanings in fine art, whose resonating effect on the cognitive faculties he equates with the feeling of beauty. Fine art can express all kinds of subjects – moral, immoral and morally neutral – and aesthetic ideas can accordingly be fitted to non-moral as well as moral subjects. There is no necessity that aesthetic ideas have a moral content.

In their very form, however, aesthetic ideas direct us towards moral awareness and a supersensible realm. As we saw in the previous chapter, aesthetic ideas in fine art are metaphor-rich images that, relative to some given theme, stimulate our imagination in a continually expansive elaboration of the theme. These themes are usually so wide, that the aesthetic ideas, although expansive, are never fully comprehensive. Consider the many artworks about war, love or intrigue, or the many paintings of the crucifixion. The resonance of the themes is endless.

The experience of aesthetic ideas in fine art is thus double-sided: the artworks' richness tends to render the given themes with a solid measure of satisfaction, while the rendition always leaves us with a sense of frustration. *Romeo and Juliet* is one of the finest tragic romances, but its excellence does not terminate the genre of tragic romance. Other tragic romances also expand upon this universal theme.

Independently of the themes expressed, and true for all aesthetic ideas, the general form of an aesthetic idea is *expansiveness* in an effort to embody a theme that defies adequate expression in a physical medium. In their very expansiveness, aesthetic ideas direct our attention away from the sensory world of images and metaphors to the conceptual sphere of reason, and thereby pave the way to morality. Kant's own examples and explanation of how aesthetic ideas in art expand our awareness are as follows:

> *The poet ventures to make sensible, realize rational ideas of invisible beings, the kingdom of the blessed, hell, eternity, creation, etc.; or even if he deals with things of which there are examples in experience, e.g., death, envy and all vices, also love, fame, and the like, he tries, by means of imagination, which emulates the play of reason in its quest after a maximum, to go beyond the limits of experience and to present them to sense with a completeness of which there is no example in nature.*
>
> (Critique of Judgement, Section 49)

Kant appreciates that although their content is not necessarily moral, the expansive format of aesthetic ideas itself extends our awareness beyond space and time to touch upon moral realities. In this respect, he believes that through its inherent expansiveness, the very format of expression in fine art is conducive to moral expression. If the form and the content of aesthetic ideas are not to contradict one another, then the content of aesthetic ideas in fine art should also be morally centred as a matter of consistency. Implicit in Kant's theory of aesthetic ideas is consequently the directive that, if we are to respect rationality, then the aesthetic ideas in fine art should have a moral content.

2 Sublimity and morality

Kant's theory of the sublime closely parallels his account of how aesthetic ideas function in fine art. He maintains that the experience of the sublime also expands our awareness – indeed, more definitively so than in fine art – into the moral realm, lifting it from the sensory into the non-sensory sphere. In the experience of the sublime this expansiveness is not caused by a metaphor-rich image, as in fine art, but by an extremely large object or a life-threatening object or situation.

The experience of the sublime in relation to extremely large objects Kant refers to as the 'mathematically' sublime, since it involves magnitudes in nature that surpass our abilities to capture them with any finite measure. The experience of the sublime in relation to life-threatening objects or situations he refers to as the 'dynamically' sublime, since it concerns nature's overwhelming power over our human bodies. In both cases we are swept away initially, either by immeasurable expanses or by immeasurable power.

When confronting a very large, seemingly endless, object or expanse – this could be either a natural expanse such as a cloud-filled sky or a human-made object such as the Great Wall of China – we try to make sense of it by holding together all of its parts in our imagination. Since the items are virtually endless, we succeed in holding in mind only some of the parts, never achieving full comprehension. The initial effect is a feeling of frustration in recognition of our imagination's weakness. We feel small in the face of the sublime.

Kant observes that our imagination, or sensory faculty, in its frustrated effort to expand sufficiently to encompass the vast object, passes its task over to a different faculty that is indeed able to complete the process of comprehension. To alleviate the feeling of frustration, the faculty of imagination's activity shifts to the faculty of reason which comprehends the object through a rational idea. The vast object may frustrate our imagination, but this frustration positively stimulates our reason, which is the seat of morality. The mathematically sublime object does not have any moral content in itself, but it acts as a stimulus to this higher awareness.

In a parallel manner, Kant observes that life-threatening objects or situations can cause an experience of the sublime. Here, the same kind of transition from our sensory-oriented faculties to our rational faculty occurs, except that there are different causes for the transition. When our physical security is endangered by terrible storms or earthquakes, for instance, and if we are not overwhelmed with fear, it becomes possible to appreciate a spiritual aspect of ourselves that remains immune to physical destruction, namely, our reason and its associated moral dimension. The experience results in a surge of moral awareness and sense of personal invulnerability in the face of death. In this respect, not only the experience of the beauty in fine art, but the experience of the sublime has a morally motivating aspect.

3 Beauty as the symbol of morality

On yet another register – that upon which we compare judgements of pure beauty and moral judgements in their elementary structure – Kant notes a further correspondence between beauty and morality. He expresses this by saying that 'beauty' – and here he intends specifically the *structure* of judgements of pure beauty – is a 'symbol' of morality. His observation is that judgements of pure beauty and moral judgements share some basic qualities, and that through this affinity, the experience of beauty invites us to draw a connection to morality.

In Kant's view, judgements of pure beauty have four main qualities that moral judgements share. First, a beautiful object pleases us *immediately* in the harmony of the cognitive faculties that it causes, and our judgement of pure beauty flows directly from that cognitive harmony. Second, the judgement of beauty is *disinterested* insofar as it is detached from worldly considerations. In particular, it abstracts from the question of whether the object of beauty is an actually existent object. Third, the judgement of pure beauty is associated with *freedom*, not in the sense of free choice, but in reference to the free play of the cognitive faculties that the beautiful object stimulates. Fourth, the judgement of pure beauty demands agreement from others, and is *universalistic*. This gives us the four qualities of (1) immediacy, (2) disinterestedness, (3) freedom and (4) universality.

Moral judgements have the same four qualities in Kant's view. First, the sense of duty that grounds moral judgements is an immediate feeling of self-respect. Second, as grounded in pure reason, moral judgements are independent of our worldly, sensory inclinations. Third, moral judgements presuppose that we are free. Fourth, they demand agreement from everyone, like judgements of beauty. In light of these parallelisms, Kant refers to beauty as a symbol of morality.

As evidence for the association, Kant mentions how in our discourse about the beauty of objects, we often cite morally toned expressive qualities, speaking, for instance, of the magnificent trees, the smiling fields, and the tender flowers. His point in drawing our attention to this style of expressive discourse, is to show that beauty and morality reinforce each other. They are the siblings of reason. Just as judgements of beauty can inspire moral awareness, moral awareness can inspire us to be more sensitive to the beauty that surrounds us:

> Now taste is at bottom a faculty for judging of the sensible illustration of moral ideas (by means of a certain analogy involved in our reflection upon both these); and it is from this faculty also and from the greater susceptibility grounded thereon for the feeling arising from the latter (called moral feeling), that the pleasure is derived which taste regards as valid for humanity in general and not merely for the private feeling of each. Hence it appears plain that the true propaedeutic for the foundation of taste is the development of moral ideas and the culture of the moral feeling; because it is only when sensibility is brought into agreement with this that genuine taste can assume a definite invariable form.
>
> (Critique of Judgement, Section 60)

4 Living things and our moral destiny

Kant's aesthetic theory occupies the first half of the third *Critique*. The second half focuses upon the principle of the purposiveness of nature and the moral meaning of the presence of living things. With respect to the principle, our cognitive faculties aim to understand nature predictably in a thoroughly mechanistic, scientific way. For this aim to be achievable, it must be assumed that nature is itself receptive to these cognitive aims as a mechanical entity through-and-through.

Kant believes that the only conceivable way for nature to be such – finding it absurd to suppose that a perfect machine of infinite extent could occur by accident – is to assume that it is the product of a divine designer, or, one could also say, divine engineer. This designer's purpose would be to create nature as a perfect mechanism, amenable to our finite minds, where each part has its own purpose within the larger systematic whole that is nature itself. Only upon this assumption does Kant believe that our scientific projects can proceed confidently and unimpaired.

Once speculation begins over the details of this divine engineer's intentions, uncertainty appears as well. It can be tempting to say that the purpose of the rain is to nourish the trees, that the purpose of the trees is to fill the air with oxygen, and that the purpose of the oxygen is to keep the animals alive, integrating each aspect of nature into an imagined system of purposes. The cited purposes can be either convincing or tenuous, but either way, they are contingent. It might seem like the purpose of rain is to nourish the trees, but rains falls in the treeless deserts and oceans as well. Even if our projections are mistaken, though, they can help us uncover mechanical connections in the world that might otherwise remain hidden, and this is Kant's point.

Key idea: The principle of the purposiveness of nature:

As rational beings we aim to know nature thoroughly as a single system of interrelated laws. This is possible, only if we assume that nature is itself amenable to our systematizing efforts. Such an assumption expresses the basic principle that everything in nature works together, just as if it were operating in view of a single purpose.

More puzzling and philosophically interesting to Kant, is yet another set of relationships that express apparent purposes in nature. These are displayed by living organisms and reveal a kind of non-mechanical causality that seems to operate side-by-side with nature's mechanical workings. We have seen in Kant's moral theory that he recognizes two kinds of causality, mechanical causality and causality through concepts, as when an architect imagines a house's plan, and subsequently constructs the house according to the plan. Of the two, the activity of living organisms more closely matches the latter kind of causality. Since most living organisms appear to lack reason, however, Kant can only explain their activity by postulating an external, divine intelligence that informs their behaviour and defines their purpose. God, so we must think, ultimately accounts for the presence of life in the physical universe.

Let us contrast mechanical causality with this non-mechanical causality which Kant discerns in living beings. One of the main characteristics of mechanical causality is its linear structure, as when, for instance, in a line of dominoes balanced on their ends, the first domino is toppled into its immediately adjacent domino, to set toppling the entire line of dominoes, one after the other.

Contrary to the image of the dominoes falling sequentially in a mechanically straight line, the behaviour of living organisms presents a more circular structure. An acorn grows into a mature oak, the mature oak itself produces acorns, and those acorns grow into other mature oaks. If we think of 'the oak' in general terms, as a species, then we could say (as Kant does) that the oak's overall movement is circular insofar as it is the cause and effect of itself over time. The oak reproduces itself to return continually in the form of a new oak tree. The dominoes in our example do not.

A comparable kind of circularity operates in the interrelationships among the parts of a living organism. In humans and other complex animal bodies, the heart supports the brain, the brain supports the stomach, the stomach supports the lungs, the lungs support the blood, the blood supports muscles such as the heart, in circles upon circles of mutual dependence throughout the organism. Kant concludes that the presence of living organisms in nature consequently requires a style of comprehension that differs from mechanical causality.

Complicating this situation, Kant finds that since their respective structures differ, the presence of living organisms confounds our scientific efforts to understand nature thoroughly and exclusively in terms of linear, mechanical causality. There is a system of organs in a living body, and a system of natural laws, but the respective structures of these systems are not obviously compatible. One is constituted fundamentally by sets of circular relationships of interdependency and self-reinforcing feedback;

the other, by sets of linear relationships that do not, as far as we can presently tell, track back or fold in upon themselves.

The circular relationships associated with living organisms are goal-oriented, for living organisms aim to sustain and reproduce themselves. Kant's observations and reflections on living organisms thus bring to a head, an apparent inconsistency between teleological and mechanical explanation. Whereas inorganic objects embody mechanical causality, organic bodies are teleological. How their respective principles fit together is a mystery.

Kant's reflections on the distinction between mechanical and teleological explanation eventually present us with two competing, grand-scale models for nature. The first regards nature as an infinitely large machine, like a clock. The second regards it as an infinitely living organism, permeated with a life force, or will. The first model is characteristic of seventeenth- and eighteenth-century Enlightenment thought. The second becomes popular with nineteenth-century German Idealistic philosophers. It also appears in some varieties of Hinduism and Buddhism.

One might ask immediately and independently which model is correct, but Kant sets the question aside as indeterminable. As the *Critique of Pure Reason* argues, it is impossible to know how things are in themselves. In Kant's view, the apparent incompatibility between mechanism and teleology is not situated objectively in nature itself, as if the world were absurd. The conflict is internal to us, and it concerns how our mind projects two opposing ways to comprehend nature as a system.

Key idea: Mechanical versus teleological explanations:

Mechanical explanations employ a linear conception of causality, as when *A* causes *B*, *B* causes *C*, *C* causes *D*, etc. Here, we would say, 'My arm raised because my arm muscles were electronically stimulated.' In contrast, teleological explanations are expressed in terms of intentions, goals or prior plans, as in 'My arm raised because I was trying to adjust the picture on the wall.'

Kant understands the apparent opposition between mechanistic and teleological interpretations of nature in reference to the tension between nature and morality: although we inhabit physical bodies that operate mechanically, our actions can nonetheless be interpreted as the effects of free choice. In relation to mechanically operating nature, the teleological structure of our living bodies and the teleological structure of our deliberate action are equally not at home. Neither seems to have a proper place in a thoroughly mechanical world.

In light of these affinities, Kant is led to resolve the tension between mechanism and teleology along the lines he adopted previously. Reiterating his rejection of all claims to metaphysical knowledge – and this includes the teleological argument for God's existence, especially salient in the present context, given how the mystery of life stimulates thoughts of God – Kant invokes the reality of our moral awareness and draws upon its philosophical implications. Specifically, he reaffirms the reality of our freedom, the consequent legitimacy of teleological styles of interpretation, and the existence of an all-good, all-knowing and all-powerful God, along with the soul's immortality, as postulates necessary to fulfil our moral duty and to achieve happiness.

Consistent with this morality-centred resolution to the problem of freedom and determinism, Kant asks what the ultimate purpose of nature might be, and states – unsurprisingly at this point – that nature's purpose is to serve as the grand platform for human moral development. Since he established in the first *Critique* that nature and freedom are compatible, he remains confident that the two conflicting styles of interpretation, mechanical and teleological, that we encounter in our observations of nature, are compatible as well.

Kant accordingly concludes the third *Critique* by reiterating the moral argument for God's existence from the second *Critique*, assuming the compatibility between nature and morality. We thus have across the third *Critique*, the *Critique of the Power of Judgement*, in Kant's discussions of pure beauty, the sublime, aesthetic ideas, beauty as a symbol of morality and the presence of living organisms, the enhancement of the compatibility between nature and morality that he earlier established. These various reinforcements lend a concrete face to the union of nature and morality that the realization of our moral destiny requires.

Spotlight: Intelligent design in contemporary thought

The Darwinian theory of evolution, which mechanically explains the emergence of new species in reference to environmental pressures in conjunction with genetic mutations, has grown popular and influential during the past century. Many also believe that life itself may have originated from the mechanical combination of inorganic compounds. Others disagree with this mechanistic orientation, asserting that living organisms are too complex to have occurred by accident, and that God, or some other form of divine intelligence, created life.

In the third *Critique*, Kant appears to agree with the creationists when he states that it would be absurd 'to hope that another Newton will arise in the future, who shall make the production of a blade of grass comprehensible to us according to natural laws which no design has ordered (*Critique of Judgement*, Section 75).

Kant, however, is merely commenting here upon a hope, consistent with the idea that a mechanical explanation of life exists beyond our comprehension. Since his philosophy is committed to the compatibility between mechanical and teleological explanation and since it resists speculating about metaphysical realities, Kant cannot be counted among contemporary creationists who assert as a matter of metaphysical truth that God created life, and who usually appeal to some version of the teleological argument for God's existence. At best, Kant is a moral advocate of creationism, fully aware that moral arguments for God's existence are weaker than the scientific or mathematical proofs that he finds unsuitable for such a metaphysical issue.

Dig Deeper

Paul Crowther, *The Kantian Sublime, From Morality to Art* (Clarendon Press, 1989)

Paul Guyer (ed.), *Kant's Critique of the Power of Judgement: Critical Essays* (Rowman and Littlefield, 2003)

John D. McFarland, *Kant's Concept of Teleology* (University of Edinburgh Press, 1970)

Robert Wicks, *Routledge Philosophy Guidebook to Kant on Judgement* (Routledge, 2007)

Rachel Zuckert, *Kant on Beauty and Biology: An Interpretation of the Critique of Judgement* (Cambridge University Press, 2007)

Study questions

1 How do aesthetic ideas direct us towards moral awareness?

2 How does the 'mathematically sublime' direct us towards moral awareness?

3 How does the 'dynamically sublime' direct us towards moral awareness?

4 In what sense is beauty a 'symbol of morality'?

5 What are the respective topics of the two main parts of the third *Critique* and how do these two parts fit together?

6 Why does Kant believe that scientific investigation requires that we assume the existence of God?

7 How are mechanical explanation, inorganic matter and linear styles of thinking related to each other?

8 How are teleological explanation, living beings and circular styles of thinking related to each other?

9 Which model of the natural world is associated with the seventeenth- and eighteenth-century Enlightenment outlook? Which model of the natural world is associated with the early nineteenth-century German Idealist outlook?

10 What is the difference between the teleological argument for God's existence and the moral argument for God's existence? Which argument does Kant advocate?

Section Five:

For what may we hope?

16

Perpetual peace as the next great step

Kant's philosophy is devoted to the proposition that our human nature is essentially moral and that through time, we can realize this moral nature in an increasingly consistent way. Up until this point, our exposition of Kant's philosophy has been primarily to show how he clears the way for freedom by restricting the scope of science to the spatio-temporal world, how he grounds his moral theory in timelessly abstract, rational principles, and how the experiences of beauty and living organisms reinforce our perceptions of the compatibility between science and morality. In this chapter, we will consider Kant's more pragmatically-oriented approach to realizing our moral nature in the world, where he formulates legislative ideas with the aim of establishing a world republic and ending war on earth. In contrast to these admirable social ideals, we will also reveal some of Kant's more questionable views in the field of anthropology.

When turning his attention to political philosophy, Kant morally reviews the course of human history – much of it painfully marked by war – and formulates legal regulations to help express, intensify and solidify the presence of rationality in society. Specifically, he sets parameters upon how rational human beings should manage basic worldly issues such as the acquisition of property, contracts, family structure, governmental structure and relationships between nations. The bulk of his reflections appear in the first half of the *Metaphysics of Morals* (1797) entitled the 'Doctrine of Right', as well as in his essay, 'Towards Perpetual Peace' (1795), both composed around the time of his retirement from teaching in 1796, at the age of 72. The doctrine of right is also sometimes identified with Kant's philosophy of law.

Kant's moral theory emphasizes that if we are to be motivated by a pure feeling of respect for ourselves as autonomous, rational beings, we must disregard instinctual inclinations, since they interferingly misdirect our attention to our contingent material bodies and person-specific physical desires. Rather than focusing upon this kind of bondage in his political theory, Kant concentrates on the bondage that groups of people impose upon one another, and attends to these more socially derived obstructions to our quest for autonomy.

In this context, Kant observes that liberation from social bondage requires that we more effectively and self-consciously direct ourselves according to our own reason, as opposed to uncritically allowing the dictates of others to determine our beliefs. In contemporary life, the external influence is recognizable in how television, newspapers and other mass media, as well as much inherited tradition, both religious and nationalistic, impress us with pre-digested viewpoints, taking the place of careful, independent reflection and analysis.

Kant does not recommend merely that individuals should do better to realize their potential to think rationally for themselves; he maintains that as a matter of civic duty, we should speak out publicly in our use of reason. If the views are rational, then they bear publicity and invite agreement. To be 'enlightened', as Kant understands the word, is self-consciously to adopt a courageous and determined, publicly oriented attitude. Given the risks that can attend publicizing the truth in the face of opposingly strong powers, he implies that courage is necessary for human moral progress.

In view of our shared humanity, it follows that those who wield potentially oppressive power ought to foster freedom of speech and active debate within the population, so that humanity as a whole can advance. Not only is it benighted to allow cowardice to precipitate one's enslavement, it is equally so to believe that in the long run, the institution of oppression is socially constructive. With such thoughts in the background, Kant states in his essay, 'An Answer to the Question: What is Enlightenment?' (1784), that the motto of enlightenment is *Sapere aude!*, 'Have the courage to use your own reason!'

Key idea: Two kinds of bondage:

Kant identifies two forces against which we must struggle to realize our freedom. The first is our animal nature, which often dominates over reason and intellect. The second is the external condition of society at large, the rules and regulations of which often assume an oppressive and objectionable form. Kant's political theory is directed towards overcoming the latter kind of bondage.

Kant nonetheless does not leave human destiny to gamble upon whether or not a critical mass of people will summon the fortitude to act rationally, or to rest on the faith that God will eventually bring everything together. He believes that, like an acorn that tends naturally to become an oak, our rational human nature tends to organize people into a reason-respecting, moral society. Although it is up to us to ensure that fear does not trump freedom, Kant speaks with a sense of inevitability that wars between nations will end and that society will progress with diminishing violence and increasing mutual respect towards a thoroughly moral, global society.

With the image of a growing organism in mind, Kant adopts a bird's-eye or cosmopolitan perspective that reveals to him some of human history's general contours. He leaves the details for others to assemble (Hegel's philosophy of world history is a prime example), but upon surveying the ancient Greeks, the Romans, the breakdown of the Roman Empire and developments up until recent times, Kant perceives a war-filled history that exhibits a gradual development in social rationality. He consequently comprehends war as a means to human development, as less enlightened societies are swept away in favour of more rationally coherent ones. Kant expresses this hard idea in the Fourth Thesis of his 'Idea for a Universal History from a Cosmopolitan Point of View' (1784):

> Thanks be to nature, then, for the incompatibility, for heartless competitive vanity, for the insatiable desire to own things and even to rule! Without them, all the excellent natural human capacities would remain sleeping, forever undeveloped. Humans want harmony; but nature knows better what is good for the species; it wills discord. Humans want to live comfortably and pleasantly; nature wills that they should be plunged from sloth and passive contentment into labour and hardship, in order to find way to extract themselves from them.

Kant refers here to 'nature', but he might have more directly referred to the divine mastermind of the natural world, for implicit in Kant's qualified support of war is a traditional response to the problem of evil: in light of God's assumed existence, evil is justified in reference to the greater good it produces in the wider scheme of things. A 'character building' response to evil appears as well in Kant's above remarks, as he asserts that without hardships, our talents and moral character would stagnate.

Despite history's violent and sorrowful road, Kant foresees an eventual end to war between nations, and he outlines a set of international regulations to promote and preserve a perpetually peaceful condition. This peaceful state of affairs is not a perfectly moral condition where lying, robbery, and other kinds of crimes that occur between individuals are absent. Perpetual peace is only a great first step that will remove one of the major causes of human suffering. After war between nations has become a thing of the past, society will need to develop morally at more specific and local levels.

Kant maintains that we can conceive of a perpetually peaceful world as built upon a set of independent republics. By 'republic', he intends a non-despotic, representative form of government where the legislative and the executive arms are managed by different people. These republics will form a league, and will respect a set of regulations that, for instance, guarantee hospitality to visiting members of foreign nations, abolish standing armies, prohibit the interference by one nation in the internal affairs of others, and prohibit the use of spies and assassins.

It may seem strange that Kant identifies perpetual peace with a league of independent republics. Given the style of philosophizing we have seen on his part, one would expect him immediately to propose a more intensely unified, one-world republic. After all, he formulates virtually all of his main doctrines in accord with the universalistic spirit of the Enlightenment, focusing almost exclusively upon unconditional constancies that apply equally to all human beings, doing his best to integrate them through a conception of reason as 'system'. His theories of human knowledge, morality and beauty display this universalistic and systematic structure.

It is a matter of debate whether Kant's political ideal is steadfastly a loose federation of independent republics or whether he also conceived of a one-world republic emerging in the longer run. From a theoretical standpoint, a one-world republic is more appropriate to Kant's persistent philosophical emphasis upon reason, which when realized, achieves total systematicity. In contrast, a league of independent republics, free to organize themselves on their own, does not obviously constitute a world-system in the strict sense, although one could imagine a global organization modelled upon the system of the human body, where each nation is analogous to a vital organ. How in real life, the nations of the world would compose themselves to operate together in such an integrated, mutually dependent way, with each serving a separate, but essential, social function in the world organization, might be more difficult to achieve than a one-world republic.

Supporting the view that a one-world republic is Kant's more distant political ideal is his complementary conception of the perfect moral community. In *Religion Within the Limits of Reason Alone* (1793), he characterizes this community as a God-governed 'universal republic based on the laws of virtue' (Book III, Part I, Section III). It is a 'kingdom of grace' or 'city of God' in the form of a universal Church to which everyone belongs. At the extremes of idealization, then, Kant presents us with two conceptions of a universal republic, one legally defined and one morally defined. Reason itself suggests their eventual integration.

When combined, these two conceptions of republic would bring the two aspects of his *Metaphysics of Morals* – the external, legal, and socially controlling doctrine of right and the moral, internal and essentially freedom-centred doctrine of virtue – into line with one another, effectively dissolving the coercive quality of the legal institutions. To appreciate this idea, imagine the difference in consciousness between following the Ten Commandments fearfully as a matter of authoritarian dictate, and following them wholeheartedly and freely as a reflection of one's own moral substance.

Situated in the role of a benevolent dictator, Kant envisions God as the governor of the ideal moral community, since only God has the insight to understand perfectly how to coordinate legality with morality. The divine role here complements how God serves more generally as the coordinator between nature and morality to guarantee the possibility of the highest good, where happiness is justly distributed.

Kant's theocratic approach to social organization, the real-world approximation of which Kant believes would call upon the religious community to govern – a community inspired and guided by the words in the Lord's Prayer, 'thy kingdom come, thy will be done, on earth as it is in heaven' (Book III, Part I, Section IV) – might not sit well with many readers. Its presence in his theory nonetheless displays the tendency towards the ideal of a one-world republic.

These considerations cast in a more pragmatic light Kant's stated advocacy of a less integrated league of nations. He can be read as prescribing the immediately necessary conditions for world peace, as opposed to describing in a perpetually peaceful world the form of government that most seamlessly exemplifies his rationalistic and systematic ideals. A variety of governmental structures is consistent with Kant's phrase, 'world republic of nations', and the social condition of perpetual peace. One of these is a relatively loose federation of states. Another is a more thoroughly integrated world republic.

Key idea: Perpetual peace:

When Kant speaks of 'perpetual peace', he is not envisioning a perfectly peaceful, heavenly, and thoroughly moral social condition. He is speaking simply and more realistically of an earthly situation where nations never go to war. He believes that ending war will dramatically transform society for the better, despite how other moral difficulties will remain to be overcome.

Although Kant's conception of reason projects us towards the ideal of a world republic in the form of a single world system, the vicious realities of present-day life render into a lofty ideal, even a loosely organized league of independent nations. As things stand, the many differences in languages and cultures upon which people's personal identities are built, require respect. Hence we can understand Kant's more realistic proposal of a league of independent republics. Since the very proposition of perpetual peace poses such a challenge to humanity, Kant's temperate advocacy of a league of nations can be regarded as an effort to realize as expediently as possible, the next great step that human society must undertake.

Spotlight: One-world government

The idea of a one-world government traces back to Francisco de Vitoria (c. 1483–1546), who, aware of the colonialist abuse of indigenous peoples in Mexico and South America, believed that the violence might end through a global institution committed to protecting people's rights – a 'republic of the entire world', as he called it. Although De Vitoria and many others have conceived of the one-world government as republican in form, the concept of such a

Kant reinforces his political philosophy with lectures and
essays on topics in anthropology and geography. Within his
philosophy, 'anthropology' is the empirical study of the human
being in its psychological and cultural context. 'Geography' is
the study of the same with respect to the natural context. Both
aim to understand realistically and historically, our capacities
for moral development. This empirical angle was important
to Kant, as he lectured on anthropology each year for almost
25 years, from 1772 until his retirement in 1796. He aimed to
present a more down-to-earth and relatively accessible rendition
of the human being based on factual evidence, complementing
his more steadfast, universalistic doctrines.

Throughout this condensed study of Kant's philosophy, we
have as a rule, adopted a sympathetic treatment of his positions
and arguments, without pressing too heavily upon any of its
conspicuous shortcomings. To put some of these undermining
aspects into perspective, we can divide Kant's philosophy into
two parts, namely, a more rationalistic and abstract segment and
a more empirically oriented segment. The bulk of his philosophy
and the segment which has been the most influential in the
history of philosophy and human culture is the rationalistic,
abstract part, where his project is to disclose universal structures
that identically govern all human beings. We have seen these in
his theory of knowledge, his moral theory and his aesthetics.

When Kant sets out to understand how well we have been
doing historically in realizing our rational nature, a library of
contingent empirical factors influences his thinking, many of
which express the limited spirit of his times. These render his
views on certain political, legal and domestic issues relatively less
convincing than what we find in other parts of his philosophy.
As a first example, consider how he asserts that 'if a man and
a woman have the will to enter on reciprocal enjoyment in

connection with their sexual nature, then they must necessarily marry each other; and this necessity is in accordance with the juridical laws of pure reason' (*Metaphysics of Morals*, Doctrine of Right, Section 24, 'The Natural Basis of Marriage'). Deciding whether or not to marry, however, as we all know, is a more complicated social matter than this rule would have us believe.

Some of Kant's lectures and short essays on anthropological topics – his lectures on physical geography, for instance – contain similarly questionable propositions, often expressive of the culture in which he lived. His views on racial and ethnic groups are probably among the most falsity-filled. He states that Native Americans are completely resistant to education, that African people can be educated, but only to be slaves, that people from the Indian subcontinent can be educated, but not in the sciences, that those who live in warmer climates tend to be lazy, that people who live in temperate zones tend to be better looking and harder working, and that the white race definitely exhibits the highest perfection of humanity. Given the empirical nature of the assertions, he might have been speaking 'to date' (i.e., the late 1700s) with respect to each, but this is uncertain.

These positions do not best constitute a reason to dismiss or ignore Kant's attempts to clothe his body of universalistic doctrine with some cultural content. They serve better as a warning shot over the bow for the reading of any theory. Like everyone, philosophers are significantly the products of their historical time period, which inevitably seeps into their outlook. Kant uses the analogy of trees that grow straight and upright when they are naturally set together within the forest without interference, suggesting that we can understand a perfectly rational social order as the upshot of similar idealized conditions. In actual forests and in the actual world, however, there is always some kind of interference.

In contrast to timeless truth, it stands analogously that historical conditions are typically laced with ignorance and oppression, working to stunt people's growth and to contort their outlooks. It might be too forgiving, but we might regard Kant's racism as an expression of the prevailing social ignorance in which he was immersed. Königsberg's location as a bustling seaport provided Kant with plenty of travelogues from which he obtained his information. The information, though, issued from a mercantile world filled with despots where aggressive colonization and the enslavement of other human beings was an established way of life. The pity of it all is that whereas the principles of Kant's moral theory are not racist, much of the information he absorbed about foreign cultures was less enlightened.

In refreshing contrast and clarity, and with a virtual step through the looking-glass, Kant was more intrigued by how propositions such as 2 + 2 = 4 are not historically conditioned. Perfectly reliable, predictable and universal in their behaviour, and setting the example for the moral theory he formulated, numbers transcend the varieties of culture and language. It is precisely here, inspired by the unchanging quality of mathematical, geometrical and logical structures, that Kant developed his most valuable contributions to philosophical thought, as he tried to be the common voice of all human beings.

With such rigorous and rigid ideals in mind, and after separating out from his consciousness, the crooked timber of his empirical constitution, he built a philosophical skyscraper out of straight and level materials, hopefully immune to historical change, and monumental for anyone who ventures to understand the nature of space, time, reason, morality and the world beyond. In this timeless achievement, he deserves our celebration.

Dig Deeper

James J. DiCenso, *Kant, Religion and Politics* (Cambridge University Press, 2011)

Patrick R. Frierson, *Freedom and Anthropology in Kant's Moral Philosophy* (Cambridge University Press, 2003)

Pauline Kleingeld, *Kant and Cosmopolitanism: The Philosophical Ideal of World Citizenship* (Cambridge University Press, 2011)

Golan Moshe Lahat, *The Political Implications of Kant's Theory of Knowledge: Rethinking Progress* (Palgrave Macmillan, 2013)

Arthur Ripstein, *Force and Freedom: Kant's Legal and Political Philosophy* (Harvard University Press, 2009)

Allen D. Rosen, *Kant's Theory of Justice* (Cornell University Press, 1996)

Study questions

1 What are some of the subjects Kant discusses in the first part of the *Metaphysics of Morals*, entitled the Doctrine of Right?

2 How does Kant's conception of enlightenment involve the need for courage?

3 Why does Kant believe that war and personal hardship can be beneficial?

4 What is the difference between a world that has achieved 'perpetual peace', as Kant understands the term, and a perfectly moral society?

5 According to Kant, through what form of governmental structure can we conceive of a perpetually peaceful world? What does he mean by the term 'republic'?

6 How does Kant characterize the perfect moral community? How does it have a religious quality?

7 What kinds of dangers are inherent in the conception of a one-world government?

8 What are some of Kant's anthropologically centred assertions about other races and ethnic groups?

9 What attraction did subjects such as mathematics, geometry and logic have for Kant?

10 In what ways do you think the contemporary historical situation in which you have been raised, has affected the beliefs that you presently have?

17

Conclusion: Kant's influence

Comparable in philosophical stature to Plato and Aristotle, Kant has made an indelible impression upon contemporary thought. In this chapter we will trace the influence of his claim that everything we know is conditioned unavoidably by our very nature as human beings. We will then consider the long-term impact of his claim that, as far as we can ever prove, rationality applies descriptively only to how ultimate reality appears to us, rather than to how it is in itself.

It is a testament to Kant's stature as a world-historical thinker that his ideas have had a constructive impact upon some of the strongest intellectual currents of the nineteenth and twentieth centuries. This is true with respect to some of his individual, more circumscribed, hypotheses and arguments, as well as his philosophical outlook as a whole. For example, as one of the early advocates of the nebular hypothesis of star and planetary formation – the thought that stars and planets are the result of gravitationally coalesced clouds of extremely tiny particles – he helped open the doors to contemporary cosmology. As a theist who nonetheless criticized the traditional arguments for God's existence, his ideas have become a mainstay within contemporary philosophy of religion. In aesthetics, with his formalistic theory of pure beauty, he inspired modernist theories of abstract art that appeared over a century later.

Even before his death in 1804, German Idealist philosophers such as Fichte, Schelling and Hegel were developing Kant's theory of knowledge and its associated conception of self-consciousness. More so than Kant, and familiar to us from Chapter 8, they appreciated how the structure of self-consciousness – a structure which Kant described rather simply in his transcendental deduction of the categories of the understanding as the 'I think' that can accompany any of our representations – harbours a fertile and paradoxical fusion of opposing components. Without Kant's philosophy to initiate their reflections, German Idealism would never have developed the notion of a dialectical fusion of opposites, and without that dialectical principle, the world would have never seen the communal, progressive vision of society that Karl Marx subsequently formulated and which became so influential in later history and politics.

As we know, one of Kant's central ideas is that all of our knowledge is affected by our very presence. Independently of our human contribution, both imaginative and limiting as it is, we can never know how the world is in itself. There have been many examples of this premier Kantian insight, some of which have appeared in the most unexpected places, such as theoretical physics. Suppose, for instance, that we want to observe something. If so, then it is necessary to shine some energy upon it, such as light waves. This works perfectly well with regular-sized objects, as our eyesight attests, but as the objects we wish to observe become smaller and smaller, there is a point at the subatomic level where the very energy that we shine upon the particles, upsets either their position or momentum. It then becomes impossible to observe any such particle as it is 'in itself', because the very act of observation disturbs the particle's condition. Although it would be optimal to be able to do so, observing an object in a perfectly untouched condition is impossible, because the only way to observe it is somehow to touch it.

In Kant's philosophy, the obstacles to our apprehension of reality as it is in itself are space, time, and the categories of the understanding, all regarded as innate ways in which we humans process sensory information. In later philosophies with a Kantian flavour, the obstacles are in the same way conceived as residing within us, but other forms and/or categories are identified as salient, taking the place of space, time and the categories of the understanding.

A fascinating example is Martin Heidegger's philosophy as expressed in his book, *Being and Time* (1927). Like Kant, Heidegger was interested in comprehending the universal aspects of the human being, although he disagreed with Kant that they reside in the structures of traditional Aristotelian logic. More practical and down-to-earth in his philosophical orientation, Heidegger sought to reveal the elements of what it is like to be a human being, not in the abstract or formalistically, but as we are situated actually and concretely in the world, walking, talking, eating, sleeping, making things and wondering about our surroundings and ourselves.

Heidegger discerned that when engaged in real-life activity with other humans, no matter where or when the human being historically happens to be, a person will, for example, have a sense of caring. The person will also have the awareness of being within and surrounded by an environment, of being in a community with other people, of being surrounded by a set of items that can be used for practical ends, of moving along a life-path where death awaits, and of wondering why we exist at all. Like Kant's categories, space and time, Heidegger's more existentially defined fundamental features of being human are universal to everyone, and define the limits of our daily awareness and possible knowledge.

Other theorists conceived of language itself as operating along the same definitive lines as Kant's categories of the understanding, space and time. Every socialized human being is nurtured to speak some language, whether it happens to be Xhosa, Greek, Thai, Uzbek, English, German, or any other of several thousand possibilities. It is amazing how children have the potentiality to learn so many languages, and in a Kantian spirit, the linguist, political thinker and philosopher, Noam Chomsky (b. 1928) hypothesized that there are innate principles for language acquisition, which in conjunction with environmental inputs, yield the different languages we speak.

More directly reflective of Kant's view that we cannot know things in themselves, however, it was further observed that each language has its own particular conceptual contours which establish for each of its speakers, the basic categories through which the world is for them divided and experienced. Insofar as languages vary, two people who speak different languages can be regarded as apprehending the world through different sets of categories.

The resulting differences in world-view between people who speak different languages can become quite pronounced. When two natural languages have respectively diverse concepts of time, or incongruent sets of colour words, or radically different grammatical structures, the speakers could be said to be living in virtually different 'worlds'. Edmund Sapir (1884–1939) and Benjamin Lee Whorf (1897–1941), an anthropologist and linguist respectively, advanced this idea of linguistic relativism in their writings. With this rendition of the basic Kantian insight, we retain the idea that our conceptual categories shape our experience, but lose the universality and commonality that Kant, Heidegger and Chomsky ascribed to their conceptions of what is fundamental to all human beings.

In accord with the idea of linguistic relativism, it follows that someone whose natural language is permeated with sexist or racist values, could also be said to live in a noticeably different world than someone whose language lacks such discriminatory aspects. Revolutionizing society can thereby be regarded significantly as a matter of changing the way people speak, where the political and moral project is to revise the vocabulary into a less prejudicial and oppressive form. An obvious example is how, in referring to everyone as a collective, we can replace the words 'man' and 'men', with words such as 'people', 'persons', 'humans' or 'humanity'. Feminist thinkers such as Luce Irigaray (b. 1930) have made considerable headway in illuminating the sexist dimensions of some of the more commonly used natural languages and in proposing alternative vocabularies.

Closely related to the theorists who regard language itself as a filter through which we apprehend the world, is yet another way to express the Kantian insight about how our conceptual categories filter our apprehension of the world. This is to maintain that not language, exactly, but the more complexly layered historical time period in which a person lives – one can call it the prevailing 'spirit of the times' – conveys its own way of apprehending the world. Inspired by this idea, Michel Foucault (1926–1984) described at some length the various styles of knowledge, along with their incongruities, that predominated respectively during medieval times, post-Renaissance times and contemporary times.

The above influences issue from Kant's fundamental idea that we must always take into account the effects of our very presence, when addressing the question, 'What can we know?' In addition, there is another way to trace Kant's historical influence – one that rests more specifically upon his idealistic position that as far as we know, the spatio-temporal world as such, has no existence independently of our minds. We have seen how Kant resolved the problem of freedom and determinism through this proposition, stating that although all of our actions in the spatio-temporal world are thoroughly predictable, freedom is still possible, because the mechanically driven, spatio-temporal world does not represent how ultimate reality is in itself.

Once we define the scientific, mathematical, predictable world of daily life as not self-subsistently real, there is a philosophical opening to assert that ultimate reality is not rational. Arthur Schopenhauer (1788–1860) expressed this view in 1818, asserting that the universe's inner reality is a blind energy that is best called 'Will', which appears in us as unconscious, instinctual energy. Extending thereby from Kant to Schopenhauer is a non-rationalist path of Kant's influence that moves from Schopenhauer to Friedrich Nietzsche (1844–1900), to Freud's psychoanalytic theory, thereafter into the early twentieth century's Surrealist artistic movement, and eventually into the literary theory of the 1960s. With respect to the pursuit of truth, these theorists tend to highlight artistic and literary methods over rationalistic philosophy, mathematics and natural science.

Among the many areas where his philosophy has had an impact, these are some of the larger historical waves of Kant's influence. As 'influences' tend to operate, they involve transformations of Kant's view, often to the point where some of his basic tenets are abandoned. The phenomenon compares to how languages slowly change as one drives across a multinational terrain, where perhaps for every 15-mile stretch, the people at each end will understand one another. After having driven 300 miles, however, the people residing at each end of the drive will be speaking entirely different languages.

From our study overall, we can now readily appreciate how it is impossible to understand our present-day historical situation well, without having an appreciation for Kant's contribution to the influential theorists who have been working for the past two centuries, numbering literally in the thousands, and extending across every major field. As one of the most important thinkers within relatively recent human history, Kant's thought has indelibly touched philosophy, psychology, politics, linguistics, physics, anthropology and theology in its emphasis upon the humility of the human condition and the supreme importance of morality.

Dig Deeper

Karl Ameriks, Nicholas Boyle and others (eds.), *The Impact of Idealism: The Legacy of Post-Kantian German Thought* [four vols] (Cambridge University Press, 2013)

Frederick Beiser, *The Fate of Reason: German Philosophy from Kant to Fichte* (Harvard University Press, 1993)

Mark Cheetham, *Kant, Art and Art History: Moments of Discipline* (Cambridge University Press, 2001)

Michael Friedman and Alfred Nordmann, *The Kantian Legacy in Nineteenth-Century Science* (MIT Press, 2006)

Tom Rockmore, *Kant and Phenomenology* (University of Chicago Press, 2011)

Further reading

Al-Azm, Sadik J., *The Origins of Kant's Arguments in the Antinomies* (Clarendon Press, 1972)

Allison, Henry, *Custom and Reason in Hume: A Kantian Reading of the First Book of the Treatise* (Oxford University Press, 2008)

Allison, Henry, *Kant's Theory of Freedom* (Cambridge University Press, 1990)

Allison, Henry, *Kant's Theory of Taste: A Reading of the Critique of Aesthetic Judgement* (Cambridge University Press, 2001)

Allison, Henry, *Kant's Transcendental Idealism: An Interpretation and Defense* (Yale University Press, 1983)

Ameriks, Karl and Otfried Hoeffe (eds.), *Kant's Moral and Legal Philosophy* (Cambridge University Press, 2009)

Ameriks, Karl, Nicholas Boyle and others (eds.), *The Impact of Idealism: The Legacy of Post-Kantian German Thought* [four vols] (Cambridge University Press, 2013)

Ameriks, Karl, *Kant's Theory of Mind: An Analysis of the Paralogisms of Pure Reason* (Clarendon Press, 1982)

Baron, Marcia, *Kantian Ethics Almost Without Apology* (Cornell University Press, 1995)

Beauchamp, Tom, and Alexander Rosenberg, *Hume and the Problem of Causation* (Oxford University Press, 1981)

Beiser, Frederick, *The Fate of Reason: German Philosophy from Kant to Fichte* (Harvard University Press, 1993)

Beck, Lewis White, *A Commentary on Kant's Critique of Practical Reason* (University of Chicago Press, 1960)

Brook, Andrew, *Kant and the Mind* (Cambridge University Press, 1994)

Buchdahl, Gerd, *Kant and the Dynamics of Reason: Essays on the Structure of Kant's Philosophy* (Blackwell, 1992)

Cassirer, Ernst, *Kant's Life and Thought*, (trans. James Haden, Yale University Press, 1981)

Cheetham, Mark, *Kant, Art and Art History: Moments of Discipline* (Cambridge University Press, 2001)

Cohen, Ted and Paul Guyer, (eds.), *Essays in Kant's Aesthetics* (University of Chicago Press, 1982)

Crowther, Paul, *The Kantian Aesthetic: From Knowledge to the Avant-Garde* (Oxford University Press, 2010)

Crowther, Paul, *The Kantian Sublime, From Morality to Art* (Clarendon Press, 1989)

DiCenso, James J., *Kant, Religion and Politics* (Cambridge University Press, 2011)

Falkenstein, Lorne, *Kant's Intuitionism: A Commentary on the Transcendental Aesthetic* (University of Toronto Press, 1995)

Føllesdal Andreas and Reidar Maliks (eds.), *Kantian Theory and Human Rights* (Routledge, 2014)

Förster, Eckart (ed.), *Kant's Transcendental Deductions: The Three 'Critiques' and the 'Opus postumum'* (Stanford University Press, 1989)

Friedman, Michael and Alfred Nordmann, *The Kantian Legacy in Nineteenth-Century Science* (MIT Press, 2006)

Frierson, Patrick R., *Freedom and Anthropology in Kant's Moral Philosophy* (Cambridge University Press, 2003)

Grier, Michelle, *Kant's Doctrine of Transcendental Illusion* (Cambridge University Press, 2001)

Gulya, Arsenij, *Immanuel Kant and His Life and Thought* (trans. M. Despalatovic, Boston: Birkhauser, 1987)

Guyer, Paul, *Kant and the Claims of Knowledge* (Cambridge University Press, 1987)

Guyer, Paul, *Kant and the Claims of Taste* (Harvard University Press, 1979)

Guyer, Paul, *Kant and the Experience of Freedom: Essays on Aesthetics and Morality* (Cambridge University Press, 1993)

Guyer, Paul, *Kant on Freedom, Law and Happiness* (Cambridge University Press, 2000)

Guyer, Paul (ed.), *Kant's Critique of the Power of Judgement: Critical Essays* (Rowman and Littlefield, 2003)

Guyer, Paul, *Knowledge, Reason and Taste: Kant's Response to Hume* (Princeton University Press, 2008)

Hudson, Hud, *Kant's Compatibilism* (Cornell University Press, 1994)

Insole, Christopher J., *Kant and the Creation of Freedom: A Theological Problem* (Oxford University Press, 2013)

Kemal, Salim, *Kant and Fine Art: An Essay on Kant and the Philosophy of Fine Art and Culture* (Clarendon Press, 1986)

Kleingeld, Pauline, *Kant and Cosmopolitanism: The Philosophical Ideal of World Citizenship* (Cambridge University Press, 2011)

Korsgaard, Christine, *Creating the Kingdom of Ends* (Cambridge University Press, 1996)

Kuehn, Manfred, *Kant: A Biography* (Cambridge University Press, 2001)

Kukla, Rebecca (ed.), *Aesthetics and Cognition in Kant's Critical Philosophy* (Cambridge University Press, 2006)

Lahat, Golan Moshe, *The Political Implications of Kant's Theory of Knowledge: Rethinking Progress* (Palgrave Macmillan, 2013)

Longuenesse, Béatrice, *Kant and the Capacity to Judge: Sensibility and Discursivity in the Transcendental Analytic of the Critique of Pure Reason* (Princeton University Press, 1998)

Louden, Robert, *Kant's Impure Ethics: From Rational Beings to Human Beings* (Oxford University Press, 2000)

Martin, Wayne M., *Theories of Judgement: Psychology, Logic, Phenomenology* (Cambridge University Press, 2006)

McCarty, Richard, *Kant's Theory of Action* (Oxford University Press, 2009)

McFarland, John D., *Kant's Concept of Teleology* (University of Edinburgh Press, 1970)

Melnick, Arthur, *Kant's Analogies of Experience* (University of Chicago Press, 1973)

Melnick, Arthur *Space, Time and Thought in Kant* (Kluwer Academic Publishers, 1989)

O'Neill, Onora, *Constructions of Reason: Explorations of Kant's Practical Philosophy* (Cambridge University Press, 1989)

Pippin, Robert, *Kant's Theory of Form* (Yale University Press, 1982)

Powell, C. Thomas, *Kant's Theory of Self-Consciousness* (Clarendon Press, 1990)

Riley, Patrick, *Kant's Political Philosophy* (Rowman and Littlefield, 1982)

Ripstein, Arthur, *Force and Freedom: Kant's Legal and Political Philosophy* (Harvard University Press, 2009)

Rockmore, Tom, *Kant and Phenomenology* (University of Chicago Press, 2011)

Rogerson, Kenneth, *The Problem of Free Harmony in Kant's Aesthetics* (SUNY Press, 2009)

Rosen, Allen D., *Kant's Theory of Justice* (Cornell University Press, 1996)

Shaper, Eva and Wilhelm Vossenkuhl (eds.), *Reading Kant: New Perspectives on Transcendental Arguments and Critical Philosophy* (Blackwell, 1989)

Shaper, Eva, *Studies in Kant's Aesthetics* (Edinburgh University Press, 1979)

Shaw, Christopher David, *On Exceeding Determination and the Ideal of Reason* (Cambridge Scholars Publishing, 2012)

Sklar, Lawrence, *Space, Time and Spacetime* (University of California Press, 1977)

Stern, Robert, *Transcendental Arguments and Scepticism: Answering the Question of Justification* (Oxford University Press, 2000)

Stuckenberg, J. H. W., *The Life of Immanuel Kant* (London: MacMillan, 1882)

Timmerman, Jens, *Kant's 'Groundwork of the Metaphysics of Morals': A Critical Guide* (Cambridge University Press, 2013)

Velkley, Richard, *Freedom and the Ends of Reason: On the Moral Foundations of Kant's Critical Philosophy* (University of Chicago Press, 1989)

Watkins, Eric, *Kant and the Metaphysics of Causality* (Cambridge University Press, 2005)

Waxman, Wayne, *Kant's Model of the Mind: A New Interpretation of Transcendental Idealism* (Oxford University Press, 1991)

Westphal, Kenneth R., *Kant's Transcendental Proof of Realism* (Cambridge University Press, 2004)

Wicks, Robert, *Routledge Philosophy Guidebook to Kant on Judgement* (Routledge, 2007)

Wike, Victoria S., *Kant's Antinomies of Reason* (University Press of America, 1982)

Wood, Allen, *Kant's Ethical Thought* (Cambridge University Press, 1999)

Wood, Allen, *Kant's Moral Religion* (Cornell University Press, 1970)

Wood, Allen, *Kant's Rational Theology* Cornell University Press, 1978

Zammito, John, *The Genesis of Kant's Critique of Judgement* (University of Chicago Press, 1992)

Zuckert, Rachel *Kant on Beauty and Biology: An Interpretation of the Critique of Judgement* (Cambridge University Press, 2007)

Index